HABITS FOR HEALING

HABITS
FOR HEALING

Reclaim Your Purpose, Peace, and Power

NAKEIA HOMER

CONVERGENT

New York

Published in the United States by Convergent Books, an imprint of
Random House, a division of Penguin Random House LLC, New York.

Convergent Books is a registered trademark and the Convergent
colophon is a trademark of Penguin Random House LLC.

LIBRARY OF CONGRESS CATALOGING-IN-PUBLICATION DATA

Names: Homer, Nakeia, author.
Title: Habits for healing / by Nakeia Homer.
Description: New York, NY : Convergent, [2024]
Identifiers: LCCN 2024016311 (print) | LCCN 2024016312 (ebook) |
ISBN 9780593727782 (hardcover) | ISBN 9780593727799 (ebook)
Subjects: LCSH: Self-actualization (Psychology) |
Burn out (Psychology) | Mental health.
Classification: LCC BF637.S4 H6443 2024 (print) |
LCC BF637.S4 (ebook) | DDC 158.1—dc23/eng/20240506
LC record available at https://lccn.loc.gov/2024016311
LC ebook record available at https://lccn.loc.gov/2024016312

Printed in the United States of America on acid-free paper

convergentbooks.com

1st Printing

First Edition

To the one who made me:
Thank you for being strong enough to wear all the heavy things that came with being a teenage mother on your back and choosing to carry and deliver me into my destiny.

To those I am called to:
Thank you for inviting me on your journey and allowing me to contribute to the work you are already doing for yourself.

Contents

HEALING MY WAY OUT

Circumstance does not make the man;
it reveals him to himself.
—James Allen, father of self-help writing and
author of *As a Man Thinketh*

At thirty-one years old, I embarked on a major life pivot when my family and I moved eight hundred miles south, from Delaware to the Metro Atlanta area. We were in search of new opportunities, new relationships, new creative energy, and ultimately a fresh start.

I was in my "new state, new me" era—eager to continue uncovering my purpose, to become a better wife, a better mother, and basically a better version of myself.

Books and YouTube videos were my teachers at the time. I must have spent a hundred hours those first few months absorbing every Zig Ziglar video or Jack Canfield book I could find. At one point, I literally ran out to my local public library to pick up *As a Man Thinketh,* the latest book I had learned about while watching a self-help lecture.

I'm not going to lie, reading that book was *tough.* Plowing through the *thinkeths, thous,* and *suffereths* was as difficult as a six-year-old trying to read (and understand) the King James Version of the Bible in Sunday school. But when I read the words "Circumstance does not make the man; it reveals him to himself," my world stood still. I finally felt *seen*. Those words helped me make sense of my entire life.

I grew up in what social workers would consider dysfunctional circumstances. My parents were fifteen and seventeen when I was born, so my paternal grandmother stepped in to foster me. My mother lived close enough that I could walk to and from her house, freely. When I was nine, my grandmom petitioned to gain custody (a necessary step so she could add me to her health insurance). One day after school, I found myself sitting in a judge's chamber, being asked who I wanted to live with. I told the judge I wanted both: my grandmom and my mom. He said I had to choose one. I picked my grandmother.

Looking back, I see my choice that day as my first major act of self-care, but it was a heavy decision for a nine-year-old to make. Many of my family members didn't understand. The order of custody was supposed to be temporary, a chance for my mom to come of age and start cultivating a home for us. It turned out to be permanent.

By the time I was seventeen, my Adverse Childhood Experiences (ACEs) score was 10, the highest one can earn. I grew up around adults who experienced depression, were in and out of prison, and were addicted to drugs and alcohol. And every time I left my mom's house, I had an overwhelming feeling of loss and rejection. Wherever I turned, I felt like I never truly belonged. There was always some reminder that I wasn't kept, chosen, or "normal."

As a child, I used to sit on the steps that led up to the door of our apartment in the projects, and daydream of a better life. I hadn't yet experienced it, but part of me hoped that I could find a life outside of the struggles I had seen in my family and community—like teenage pregnancy, drug addiction, domestic violence, and poverty. I believed if I committed myself to doing things differently, I'd eventually experience it.

Over time, I came up with a strategy: I would do the opposite of every bad habit I saw around me. That's all my little mind could think of at that age. The overtly bad habits were obvious: Say no to drugs, stay away from men who were controlling and aggressive, and get a good education. It seemed simple enough. But on a deeper level, I was unaware of the catch: Having to grow up fast, take on grown-up duties, and navigate pressures even the adults in my life couldn't handle put me in a constant state of survival mode. Eventually, that pressure had its consequences. I became tough and verbally aggressive. I grew hypervigilant and overly sensitive to the needs and wants of family members with addictions. Every moment of struggle felt like something I needed to overcome—not just for me, but also for the family members and friends who couldn't.

Today, I am a first-generation college graduate, working as a mental well-being professional, business owner, and author. I made it out of the hood, physically. I broke generational cycles of abuse, poverty, and addiction. But my upbringing left scars that I've spent the majority of my adult life working through and trying to heal. Guilt and shame clung to me as I tried and failed to save family members from hardship. I became an overachiever, the kind of person who worked, studied, and researched, and left no room for a social life. This led to serious burnout, migraines, lower back pain, digestive problems, and other stress-related issues. My day-to-day was dictated by a constant fear that something bad was going to happen.

When I was earning my degree in psychology, my textbooks and lectures contained no mention of "healing" those habits I had developed over the years. We were taught about diagnosing, coping, and predicting outcomes but given little to no information on how to help restore and mend survivors back to a place of mental and emotional health and well-being.

I wanted more. I wanted to build a life that had room for me to *just be* without struggle, without the lack of security and stability, and without the lingering habits of trauma. I wanted to uncover my gifts, explore my talents, and choose a path driven by joy and pleasure. I wanted to know what it felt like to walk through a safe neighborhood and someday cultivate a functional family dynamic of my own. I wanted to replace worry, hardships, and chaos with peace, power, and purpose.

Your circumstances might be different from mine, but I'm guessing you know what it's like to be at war with a pattern or cycle. Maybe you are honest about your trauma, but you think that because it's in the past, you are "okay." You've moved on. Or maybe you're conscious of the emotional bruises and scars you still carry. You know that you can't change the past, but now that you are on the other side of it, you're struggling to change the habits and the mindsets you had to develop to survive it.

I wonder if, like me, you've been on a mission to set things right in your life. Maybe you've worked hard so you would never be broke again. Maybe someone hurt you, and you've developed thick skin so that wouldn't happen again. Maybe you've learned how to let things slide, how to shelve certain issues, and how to ignore simmering conflict because you are tired of negativity sucking the energy out of your life. Or maybe you went out of your way to prove you were different from the people who hurt you, and now you feel like the black sheep of the family.

People like us are riddled with burnout, emotional exhaustion, toxic relationships, somatic symptoms (like headaches, back pain, digestive issues, and even hair loss), and spiritual unrest. Living in survival mode has its consequences. *The habits that you used to survive your past may be the cause of your current pain.*

Habits for Healing extends an invitation for you to take back control of your life. Your past or your current circumstances may have upset you, hurt you, confused you, or caused you to do things you never thought you'd do—but they didn't *make you*. It's your habits that are to blame for where you are today.

Forming a habit is inevitable. You may have heard that people are "creatures of habit." We are biologically wired to repeat behaviors that meet our needs, and this mechanism is designed to sustain us.

But this process of forming habits isn't always a conscious one. You can repeat a behavior without even realizing it—like getting the same haircut for ten years or eating a whole bag of chips when you're stressed. It's even possible to activate a default response to something you experienced before—like saying "good" when someone asks how you're doing (even when you're not good) or working late every night to avoid an argument with a partner with mood swings. People develop countless habits in split-second moments or during complex experiences, and those habits can grow into behaviors and eventually evolve into values.

The habits we will work to heal in this book are the behaviors you've developed, often early in life, to manage struggles, hurts, or setbacks. To push through those experiences, you began to respond in ways that helped you protect your heart, keep the peace, and survive. And because those behaviors served you at the time, you set them on repeat. They then became your automatic responses to similar experiences or any perceived threat to your well-being. So, you've managed to get this far in life giving little thought to how the habits that once served you are now making things happen that you don't want.

Listen, this is in no way a diss. You did what you were supposed to do! You made it through, out, and over to the other side—and hear me when I say *I see you*. And now your habit of trying to survive your circumstances may have revealed some telling things about who you are and how you show up in the world.

You're a survivor.

You're *the strong friend.*

You know how to get things done.

You don't ask for much.

. . . You're also exhausted.

Hustling to build a life and career, guarding your heart, holding on to what you love for dear life, or being a rescuer may have served you in the past. But here you are now: Discontented with what your life has become, and longing for fulfillment, freedom, and autonomy. Longing for peace, purpose, and power.

Maybe you're at a crossroads: You're lacking the motivation to do things differently or you've accepted that your life will always be hard; but there is a part of you that is still holding out hope that life can get better.

Listen to me. You are right.

Life can get better.

HABITS FOR HEALING

In this book, we will consider the negative habits you may have missed on your journey, or the fears you are struggling to heal. We'll uncover the story behind your mindset. We'll address sources of beliefs and behaviors that make you resistant to change. We'll look at how not prioritizing yourself, not setting boundaries with family and friends, not being able to let things go, being too hard on yourself, and taking things personally are all keeping you from becoming the person you are meant to be. We'll shift from habits for survival to habits for healing, which will push you closer to the meaningful life you deserve.

In part one, Reclaim Your Purpose, we'll examine habits that will help you identify your needs, release things that limit your well-being, and develop the courage you need to take back ownership of your own life.

In part two, Reclaim Your Peace, we'll consider habits that help you move away from things you can't control, improve your self-esteem, and free you from dependence on acceptance and approval from others.

In part three, Reclaim Your Power, we'll explore habits that you can leverage to focus on what matters, improve your relationship with yourself and others, and stand in the truth of who you are.

You'll read a mixture of stories from my own life and from clients I've worked with throughout my career. By sharing the circumstances that helped shape me, I hope to inspire you to own your journey, so you can decide on the direction of the stories that have yet to be told. And as for my clients, every story is real, but all identifying information (names, ages, and timelines) has been changed to protect their privacy.

As you read, I want to encourage you not to downplay your traumatic experiences if they don't seem as dramatic as mine or those of someone else you know. Bad breakups, growing up with emotionally unavailable adults, being bullied by friends or siblings, or being treated poorly based on your abilities, skin color, gender, or core beliefs are all experiences that require healing.

You can see the unfortunate circumstances you've experienced as just a chapter in the story of your life and fill the rest of your pages with stories of overcoming, healing, and growth. Remember that your circumstances didn't make you—your habits did. Every unhealthy habit can be replaced with a new and healthy one. You can decide, at this moment in your life, to do things differently.

Each healing habit and practice in this book is intentionally designed to empower you to transform the relationship you have with your past, your future, yourself, and with others.

I'm so proud of you for honoring the pieces of yourself that are rooted in the hope that life can be so much better.

Keep believing that you will experience it.

HABITS FOR HEALING

PART ONE

RECLAIM YOUR PURPOSE

Refuse to inherit dysfunction. Learn new
ways of living instead of repeating what
you lived through.
—Dr. Thema Bryant

Chapter 1

THE HABIT OF SELFISH TIME: HOW SELF-CARE HEALS OUR RELATIONSHIP WITH WORTHINESS

I take the long way home from every destination I can. From the grocery store, the post office, dropping the kids off, the gym—each drive is an opportunity for me to just be with myself. The music or podcast is up as loud as it can go. Phone conversations with my friends are spicy, juicy, and full of details only safe to be shared in the car. Some rides are silent, and some rides are just for tears. I think. I lament. I hold space for myself. During some of my sacred rides alone, I've written songs, poems, and prose through voice notes. I've even practiced keynotes, telling an employee I was letting them go, and how I was going to explain to my son why I ate all the candy I told him he couldn't have.

Every drive counts. Once I walk through the door to my home, I am no longer just with myself. Even if I get only ten to fifteen more minutes alone, I savor these moments in the car when I get to do whatever I feel like doing. For years, this was my only real self-care practice. Now, it sits at the top of my list.

I didn't see driving as self-care at first. I didn't even realize this was a pattern until life got busy or I just stopped prioritizing the habit. When I felt anxious, I'd hop in the car and go for a drive.

When I needed to think something through, I'd hop in the car and go for a drive. When I wanted to be alone for a while—surprise, surprise—I'd hop in the car and go for a drive. Because so much of my life was about taking care of other people, these bouts of me time in the car became a way to recharge. When I took time to be by myself, I had enough gas in the tank to engage in the other responsibilities I had committed to. But when I didn't, my anxiety, tension, and burnout would only persist, eventually taking a serious toll on my mood, how I engaged with my family, and my workflow.

Eventually, I had to think deeper about why the habit of taking these solo drives was so important to me. And if it was so important, why did I deprioritize that time whenever someone else needed something from me or to give attention to things that didn't nourish me?

WHAT SELF-CARE IS

Self-care is a habit that enhances your overall well-being. It's any routine, practice, or sacred choice that you do only for yourself, that keeps you mentally, physically, and spiritually healthy. Self-care helps you realize your full potential, cope with daily stressors, keep up with responsibilities, and even maintain relationships with friends and family. Self-care sets us up for not only internal success but also external success, by filling our cups with the energy and nourishment we need to pour into the lives of others.

What I've come to deeply love about self-care is that it is a habit you can tap into with or without the participation of anyone else. It's an accessible in-the-moment or anticipating-the-future habit. You don't need a professional guide to self-care, you don't need a self-care budget, and there isn't a self-care limit.

Years ago, I discovered I had a natural resistance to self-care. I had internalized harmful messaging from my past that sprang to mind whenever I prioritized habits like my solo drives. A voice inside me insisted: *My needs are not as important as the needs of others. Time alone is for single people with no children. A good person always puts others before themselves. Self-care takes all day.*

Sound familiar?

These narratives were keeping me from experiencing a harmonious and well-functioning life, and I knew something needed to change. I wanted to embrace a healthy habit of self-care, and I also wanted to sustain it. To do that, I first needed to understand where the roots of my internal resistance were coming from.

FIRST LESSONS IN RESISTANCE TO SELF-CARE

Every day I watched my grandmom leave for work before daybreak and return after sunset. She would wake me up to say my prayers. She had two ways of getting me up, one with a singsongy "Kei, time to get up," and the other by singing an old church hymn with her distinct soprano voice. On days my grandmom was overwhelmed with various things—health issues, bills, or the literal highs and lows of the two active drug users in her home—I'd hear her praying alone in the mornings. From the gap underneath the bathroom door, I heard her begging God for strength to endure it all. I'd get washed up and dressed for school, and then lie back down on the couch to rest a little more, watching as she walked out the door of our apartment in the projects, headed to her first job of the day.

I was what is known as a latchkey kid. Every morning before she left for work, my grandmom tied a house key to a green string that I kept around my neck. From kindergarten on, I was responsible for getting myself to and from school.

My grandmom worked no fewer than two jobs at once. By the time I was in middle school, she had taken on a third. She ran her own catering business on top of it all, and she also volunteered as our church's cook—a role she was known for throughout the entire community. There was a joke around town that people would show up during the final moments of the church service just so they could indulge in my grandmom's cooking. The smell of foods like roast beef and collard greens permeated the streets surrounding our church on the corner of South Pine and Willow. A small highway separated our church from the local KFC, but my grandmom's chicken was what everyone raved about. Come rain or shine, in sickness or in health, tired or energized, paid or not, my grandmom went to work.

I watched her work long hours, day in and day out, until she was in her mid-sixties. By that time, she suffered from high blood pressure, diabetes, asthma, back surgeries, carpal tunnel syndrome, several strokes, and a heart attack. She walked with the cutest bowlegged limp that I'm certain was painful, but she never complained.

Around my senior year of college, my grandmom was forced into retirement. For years, she had been working for a nonprofit agency as a cook that provided meals for daycares. Every day, starting at 5 A.M. and ending around 6 P.M., she prepared breakfast and lunch for hundreds of children. Eventually, her employer noticed the toll that her work was taking on her body. He offered her an executive position that would allow her to hire and train additional staff and delegate the duties she had been performing solo for years. But my grandmom was a hands-on kind of woman. She couldn't just stay out of the kitchen. When her employer came back with an ultimatum to either supervise others or retire—she chose the latter. And when she finally sat down, she struggled to get back up, both literally and figuratively.

My grandmom was amazing at taking care of her family and neighbors. She was an advocate for me and other at-risk youth in our community, an advocate for survivors of domestic violence, and a national advocate for equitable education for underserved communities—and she did all of that at the expense of her own well-being.

I asked her once if she would go back and do things differently if she could, and she answered with the swiftest "no." My grandmom left a beautiful legacy, which I dare not diminish. She did what needed to be done to survive, and she did what she was called to do as a woman of service. That woman taught me about love, she taught me about God, she taught me about being of service to others, and so many other beautiful things—she just taught me nothing about self-care.

For years, I internalized that helping others was defined by giving up everything you had and going as hard as you can. Later on, when I learned about the concept of self-care, I thought it was something I might be able to earn—only if there was time and energy left over from what I gave to everyone else. I quickly realized that that approach was unsustainable. Not only did I never have enough time or energy left over for myself, but I also began to resent how I chose to spend it on others. The consequences of my choices began to materialize as burnout, anxiety, depression, and an overwhelming feeling that I had no purpose outside of what I did for others.

We do what we see done.

The behavior of adults we looked up to in our homes inevitably set the tone for our own earliest behaviors. If we are conditioned to see selfless acts as the only definition of being a good person, then the habit of service, even at the expense of our own health, finances, and mental well-being, will start to define us. In our quest to be seen as a kind and dependable person in the lives of those we love, we abandon our duty to love and care for ourselves in the same ways.

SOCIETAL BARRIERS TO SELF-CARE

We now live in a time when some types of self-care are trendy. Parents are encouraged to get a sitter and go out for a date. The ladies are getting together for girls' nights out and Sunday brunches. Brunch is preferred.

Interestingly enough, there is still a struggle to do those things consistently and without feeling guilty. The biggest complaint I hear about self-care is that people don't want to spend the money or the extra time. Brunch is fun, but it's costly. Between the dress, the shoes, the perfect restaurant, and parking, that kind of self-care can be an investment in the hundreds if you're indulging every weekend. Another example is that parents who want to go out for date night struggle not to spend the evening talking about the kids, checking in on the kids, and rushing back home to the kids. It's as if every other role we play in life cannot coexist with parenthood. Because those date nights are no longer as fiery and fun as they were before we became parents, they tend to happen less often.

Do you ever feel the urge to shift away from wonderful yet surface-level self-care, like getting your nails done or indulging in a massage? Do you ever feel a longing for something more serious or honest, like setting boundaries or going to therapy? If you've tried the trendy dates and brunches and still feel guilty, or you feel that self-care is not worth the investment, it's because those practices are not supporting an underlying need. You may need more support around the house, time alone to ideate or rest, or help uncovering values that make you feel aligned with your purpose.

For self-care to be effective, it must meet a need that enhances your life.

So, I want to challenge you to reframe your current surface-level self-care and consider how it might meet a deeper need—something that fosters connection and feels sustainable. Instead of waiting for date night, what if you tried thirty minutes of connecting with your spouse after the kids go to bed each night, and discussed tasks you could support each other on that would take a load off your plate for the week—like taking turns packing school lunches? Or what if instead of rallying your squad to go to costly brunches every weekend, you tried calling a friend on your commute home from work one day to talk through your desire to go back to school and earn a degree?

Sometimes it feels like we're all juggling the world. I get that. On days that I'm bouncing back and forth between parenting, working, cooking, cleaning, and being present in all my relationships—while trying to do this from a place of healing and growth on top of that—I can get a little dizzy. But what I'm confident of is this: None of these responsibilities could happen if I wasn't making sure to build a foundation of recovery time, rest, and self-reflection.

Let's just say I am not my grandmom. Though I decided early on to be a woman of service, I decided not to sacrifice my well-being to do it. It took some time, reprogramming, and intentional effort, but I have redefined what it means to be a good woman—and I love it here.

Now, I said I love it here, but staying here is not easy. Sometimes I am tempted to honor my commitment to others above my commitments to myself.

I often describe my daughter as one of my greatest teachers. She was born when I was twenty-six, but since I didn't grow up with a traditional mother-daughter relationship, I had a lot of insecurities about the mother-daughter dynamic. How would I learn to create the bathtime or bedtime traditions I wanted my daughter and me to experience? How would I manage my professional aspirations while still being present for my family? I was so afraid I would mess it up, and I had to do a lot of healing while she was growing up.

One day during our 7:30 P.M. sessions—a time when she talks with me and I make a point to listen—I asked her if there was anything she thought I could do differently or better. She was eleven or twelve years old at the time. I expected her to say, "You could buy me more things," or, "You could take me more places," but instead, my brilliant human being of a child said: "You could be less selfless. Like, you don't have to sacrifice everything all the time."

What?!

I said that out loud. Literally.

She explained, "You don't have to give us your last bit of food or candy. You can go places without us and do things you like. You can think about yourself sometimes." She was still a kid, at an age of development when we're programmed to think about ourselves, but she was experiencing me doing what I thought was the best thing for her and her little brother as *too much.* I thought I was being the mother I never had, the mother she needed me to be. But I was actually projecting an unhealthy, unspoken message about self-care onto her.

That day, I committed to practicing a new version of motherhood. Moving forward, on weekdays before the kids woke up, I started practicing a self-care morning routine. I spent Saturday mornings with myself and even carved out time to soak in the tub, uninterrupted, each night after dinner. I started watching my favorite shows again and listening to music I enjoyed during drives in the car. (This is when the habit of taking the long way home was born.) I made sure that some of these were visible practices that my kids could witness; I wanted their first lessons in self-care to be healthy ones.

But let me be clear: *You do not have to be a parent or have a family to be deserving of self-care.* You may be an advocate for others, the strong friend in your circle, the go-to problem solver, or the model employee in the office. Most of us have more than one identity. All of those roles will stretch you in ways that still require deliberate care.

This truth became clear to me when working with Lisette, a twenty-four-year-old traveling nurse who was a first-generation college graduate and the first one in her family to venture out of their home state.

> Not having children or a family doesn't mean you
>
> * Don't need time alone
> * Have unlimited time to devote to others
> * Don't feel tired or depleted
> * Don't need time to prepare for each day
> * Can stay up all night
> * Don't have financial obligations
> * Are obligated to babysit the children of your siblings or friends
>
> You have a right to take care, too.

Lisette was also the first one in her family to achieve what they all considered success, but she knew that her family's emotional, spiritual, and occasional financial support had contributed to making her position possible, so she felt a responsibility to give back.

Whenever family members would ask for money to help pay bills or buy necessities, Lisette would oblige. She was pressured to take trips back home for birthdays, anniversaries, and the births of nieces and nephews. It got so intense that even when someone in her family just wanted time away, Lisette was asked to fly them to her city, and put them up for days, even months, on her own dime.

Lisette didn't mind helping. But what started out as giving back turned into an obligation to support multiple family members financially and physically. This obligation came at the expense of her own life and needs. In addition to student loan debt, Lisette started racking up credit card debt, just to keep up with the needs of others.

These financial pressures took a toll on Lisette's mental and physical health. She carried guilt, resentment, and stress on her back, working sixteen-hour shifts just to keep up. She started experiencing weight gain, back pain, and headaches. And eventually, her relationships with family members became strained.

In our sessions, Lisette's first step toward self-care was to unlearn the messages she'd received. She learned that self-care wasn't something you had to earn after a lifetime of hustling to be successful. She learned that being single without kids didn't mean she had to be available all the time. Finally, she learned that allowing others to exploit her was a debt she wasn't obligated to pay simply because she was the first to break generational cycles of struggle. Eventually, Lisette came to realize that prioritizing her own health and well-being was paramount for her to maintain the livelihood that was sustaining her and her family.

After a family meeting where she shared the changes she'd be making—like implementing a personal budget, limiting visits back home, and taking some time away from everyone to de-stress and recover—Lisette was surprised to learn that everyone was in full support of her new self-care practices. Her family had always genuinely cared for her and so when she drew a line, they respected it.

WHY SELF-CARE MATTERS

Starting your healing journey with the habit of self-care is important because you're laying a foundational, sustainable habit that prioritizes your mind, body, and soul. It might seem selfish to prioritize your needs before anything else, but this habit gives us the bandwidth to begin healing other areas in our lives. When your mind is healthier, you think with more clarity, make better choices, and start to build the life you want. When your body is healthier, you have the physical ability, energy, and freedom to move through life with ease and confidence. When your soul is healthier, you experience the self-awareness, spiritual insight, and emotional fortitude that allows you to connect with others more deeply. Self-care is a beautiful habit that allows us to witness how healing ourselves heals others as well.

Self-Care Sets the Tone for Sustainable Healing

Many of us struggle with self-care because we start trying to practice it when we're already in survival mode. By the time we are working to be intentional, we are physically sick, emotionally exhausted, and spiritually depleted. Instead of choosing healthy habits, we see them as this thing we *have to do* to recover from a crisis, or a last-ditch effort to not completely fall apart.

Self-care is not only restorative, but also preventative. The habit of meeting your needs consistently prevents many mental and physical emergencies—making self-care something you do because it enhances your life, not just saves it. Inspired self-care feels so much better than prescribed aftercare.

Self-Care Is Community Care

There was a time in my childhood when I thought my grandmom hated me. Yes, I'm talking about the same woman who exhausted herself making sacrifices for me. I was a preteen, experiencing involuntary mood changes and still trying to make sense of my relationships with my mom and dad. My grandmom was working hard, taking care of me and the additional family members that were now living in our small apartment. Things were tight financially and physically. The pressure built on my grandmom until she couldn't take it anymore.

I started working under the table at a local beauty supply store at twelve years old. It got me out of the house for a few hours, and I gave the $35 I got paid each week to my grandmom to help buy food or a tank of gas. In those years, my grandmom would often get a little moody in her tone toward me. Other times she was just outright mean. I couldn't understand it.

When I read my diary entries from back then, it makes me sad. I wrote things like *Grandmom isn't talking to me again. The silent treatment feels worse than getting a beating. I wish I could make more money right now. My grandmom wouldn't be so stressed out if she didn't have to pay for everything for me on her own.*

But she was different on the train we took from Philadelphia to West Palm Beach or Miami, Florida, during the summer, or on the drive from New Jersey to Michigan during winter break. We would sing songs together. I would see her laughing and telling stories. She would get dressed up and put on her best costume jewelry. My grandmom seemed to be a totally different version of herself when she was away from the day-to-day stuff, visiting family and friends. Now that I'm older, I recognize the difference between my *exhausted* grandmom and the *well-rested* version of her—the grandmom who was in survival mode and the grandmom who had a few weeks in Florida every summer, to thrive. When she had time to take care of herself, our relationship was always better.

What if I told you that you are worth just as much when you are resting as you are when you are working? Do you even know what being at your best looks and feels like?

I believe you have an obligation to yourself and to the people who love and count on you to be your best. Modeling the habit of what it means to be a good person can break a generational cycle of self-sacrifice and introduce a whole new way of being.

If you're honest, maybe you would admit you've used a hundred reasons to neglect yourself. Maybe you are single with no children. Maybe you have to work hard to pay off debt. Maybe you feel a responsibility to give back to your family. And here's the thing: You can do all of these things. Just not at your expense. I challenge you to remain the thoughtful, present, and dependable person that you are *and* be sure to share some of those qualities with yourself.

Reserve some of the goodness *in* you *for* you, too.

Two things to remember:
Self-care is not me only; it's me *too*.
Self-care is not me only, but it may mean me *first*.

WHAT SELF-CARE HEALS IN US

On an episode of her *Homecoming* podcast, Dr. Thema Bryant explained the source of our reluctance to take care of ourselves: "If you loved yourself, some of the things you've been deliberating over would be an easy choice." I must have played back that sentence fifty times. In most realms of our lives, deliberation—or careful consideration and thought—usually happens *before* action is taken. You deliberate and decide what you want for dinner. You deliberate and decide where to go on your next vacation. You deliberate (for what seems like an hour, if you're like me) and decide on the color for your next mani-pedi. When you are deliberate, you are conscious, you are intentional, and you are careful.

Imagine what your life would be like if you were conscious and careful about the habits you practice to enhance your well-being.

Sit with that thought for a moment.

Does choosing to care for yourself come easily for you? How would you feel if you started practicing those things before it was too late?

When you're deliberate about your self-care, it might sound like this:

- I recognize that I need more time to just be with myself because I am feeling stretched and depleted.

- I am aware of my responsibilities to my family, but I am also responsible for myself.

- I commit to actually taking a twenty-minute lunch break a few times a week.

- I commit to reserving an additional thirty minutes to run errands alone on the weekends.

- I commit to an earlier bedtime for the kids, so I can use the extra time to recover in the evenings.

Thinking about your needs and wants may seem selfish at first. But eventually you and everyone you are connected to will benefit from it.

Only you know your current circumstance. Only you know

what you need in this season of your life—and that is exactly where to begin cultivating the healing habit of self-care.

THE INTERSECTION OF SELF-CARE AND SELF-LOVE

My introduction to self-love went like this: "Look in the mirror and repeat the words *I love you* ten times." The idea was to repeat this practice, every day, until you believed it, meant it, and felt it.

I was in search of something deeper than just loving my body and feeling beautiful. I wanted to love and value my time and energy. I needed to love the decisions I made that may have upset my family a little. I wanted to not feel guilty for choosing things that were best for me—even when it meant there would be distance between me and those I loved.

When you view self-love through the lens of self-care, you give yourself permission to engage in acts of self-love, not just say the words. Loving yourself could mean you don't have as much free time for other people because you are spending it reading books, watching videos, and engaging in other habits that will help you develop personally. Self-care is how you *show* yourself love.

I have demonstrated how self-care positions you to care for others. But please know that you deserve self-care just for you. These days I love myself by creating a daily schedule for me and my family, asking for help when I need it, texting or calling one of my good friends throughout the day, going to sleep at 9:30 most nights, and setting reminders to drink a glass of water every two hours. I don't have to earn these deliberate acts of self-love, and I don't do them only if I have extra time. Just as brushing my teeth and washing my face are essential in my daily routine, so is drinking my morning cup of coffee in silence every morning and leaving everyone at the dinner table to go soak in the bathtub at night. My self-care habits are built into the fabric of my daily life.

SELF-CARE AND YOUR PURPOSE

Generally speaking, your purpose is your reason for existing. But when we fixate on things in our lives that are outside of our control, we limit what our purpose could be. That's why for me, it's essential to approach purpose in a way that centers sustainable, nourishing self-care.

People often label their purpose as their job, being a parent, being a partner, or fulfilling some duty to others. But your job and career are subject to conditions you don't always determine, and they can feel stagnant or evolve at certain points in your life. Also, the role you play in the lives of others requires their consent, and can sometimes end abruptly, or against your wishes. We outgrow people, places, and things, which makes it difficult to assign purpose to them indefinitely.

After being on the journey to purpose for more than four decades, and working with others to uncover theirs, I have come to define purpose as *becoming the best version of yourself.* Your purpose is to exist in the fullness of who you are, in every moment and season of your life, as best you can. *Self-care is the habit that helps you meet your personal best.* Every time you engage in daily practices, rituals, and acts of self-love, you are practicing a sustainable system of affirming and meeting your own needs. When you take care of yourself, you reclaim your purpose.

FIVE MORE SELF-CARE HABITS
FOR BEING AT YOUR BEST

1. **Indulge in one thing that's just for you.** Take yourself to dinner or a movie or buy a snack or luxury skin-care item that is meant only for you. Show yourself that you are deserving of good things.

2. **Set a timer to take three deep breaths every three hours.** You'll be amazed at how doing this consistently can decrease stress over time. This is a preventative habit, but also one you should use while experiencing a difficult day.

3. **Schedule a daily check-in with your emotions by asking, "How do I feel?" and "How do I want to feel?"** Do this every morning before you start your day or in response to sudden mood changes to regain control of your emotions. When you identify a feeling, assign one self-care action to address it, and commit to taking that action before the end of the day.

4. **Harness the power of nostalgia in your day by looking at old photos or listening to old songs.** These habits release feel-good hormones, act as a healthy distraction, and can improve relationships when you do them with someone you love. This is also a great practice if you forget what it felt like to be at your best. Remembering where you were, what you were doing, and who you were with when you were at your best in the past can inspire you to re-create versions of those things now.

5. **Try releasing tension by taking a few minutes to give yourself permission to cry, scream, or even shake your body rhythmically or vigorously.** Avoiding or denying your true emotions contributes to poor well-being, but physically processing them leads to emotional clarity and calm. We are taught that outward expressions of internal emotions are signs of weakness or poor mental health, when the truth is they are signs of emotional maturity.

PROMPTS FOR SELF-CARE

What do you need at this moment? What are your biggest complaints when it comes to how you spend your time and energy? What do you feel pressured to do for others at your expense? What has your mood been like? Has a lack of self-care negatively impacted your relationships?

Why do you need it? Knowing why can give you the permission you've been waiting for.

What will your self-care habits look like? Do you need a new schedule? Can you delegate some of your responsibilities? Do you need to unlearn old behavior models?

How will you practice the habit of self-care today, this week, and/or this month? What actions can you commit to doing? List at least one thing you can do immediately. It could be something as small as putting your phone on Do Not Disturb while you read or journal for fifteen minutes, or as big as declining the extra shift at work this weekend. Can you build in time to stretch before getting started with your day? Or do you need to do something more long-term, more reflective, like redefining what you being a good person looks like?

USE THE SPACE BELOW TO WORK
THROUGH THE PROMPTS ON YOUR OWN

Need: _____

_____

_____

Why do I need to do this? _____

_____

_____

Healing Habits: _____

_____

_____

Practices/Action: _____

_____

_____

AFFIRMATIONS FOR SELF-CARE

Say this out loud with me:

I am deserving of tender love and attention.

I won't wait until there is an emergency to take care of me.

I will take care now.

Well is a glorious thing to be.

I am creating a new legacy of positive well-being and purpose.

Caring for myself improves my capacity to care for others.

Chapter 2

THE HABIT OF EDITING YOUR LIFE: HOW LETTING GO HEALS OUR RELATIONSHIP WITH CHANGE

I am good at throwing away things I don't like or no longer want, but that skill pretty much evaporates when the belonging means something to me—even if it's broken. I didn't realize that about myself until I was sitting in an emergency room in my twenties, thinking about how I ended up there.

It all started seven years earlier, with a last-minute trip to the fanciest department store I knew at the time: Macy's. My grandmom took me there to look for shoes for the prom. Having just gone through a breakup, I had initially sworn off prom, along with anything else that reminded me that I no longer had a boyfriend. But in the final hour (meaning the deadline for purchasing tickets), a friend convinced me to go, saying I'd look back and regret not having this memory. So, I bought two prom tickets—one for me and one for the date I had yet to secure—and started looking for the most important part of the night: my shoes.

I knew the style of shoe I was looking for and was certain Macy's would have it. I was right. I found the perfect pair immediately. They were black, satin, strappy, and adorned with just the right number of rhinestones to make them look expensive but not cheesy. I asked for my size and tried them on, striding from mirror to mirror a few times to make sure I could walk in them comfortably. I didn't even have to ask for my grandmom's opinion. She nodded in approval as soon as I picked them up. (I inherited my love of shoes from her. She had kitten heels in every color and style.)

Despite my initial hesitation, I went to the prom and didn't regret it. I spent most of the night dancing, and I went home feeling grateful I'd listened to my friend.

Those expensive-looking shoes went back into the box and saw the light of day on just two other occasions. The first time I put them back on, I felt a slight wiggle every time I took a step. And on the second occasion the heel broke. But I quickly fixed it, promising myself that I would retire the shoes *eventually.* Seven years later, when I was hosting a fancy concert for one of our clients, I pulled the shoes out a third time.

On the day of the event, I remembered only that the shoes perfectly matched my dress, forgetting my earlier promise to myself to throw those unstable heels away. The outfit was complete, the event was a success, and it was only on the way out, down a two-story flight of stairs, that I stepped down on the temporarily fixed heel and broke my ankle.

You may have heard the expression "let go or get dragged" before. This was a "let go or fall" moment.

During the hours I spent waiting in the ER, I realized that I had held on to those old shoes from prom because they were symbolic of something deeper. They were a tangible reminder that I knew how to move on from heartbreak. They were proof of my resilience. Which is why I couldn't let them go until they put me in literal, physical danger.

WHAT LETTING GO MEANS

Letting go as a concept is not always as straightforward as the habit of self-care. But as a practice, it is simply relinquishing your physical, mental, or emotional grip on some*one* or some*thing* when it is no longer in your best interest to hold on.

Letting go is ending a relationship with someone you are no longer compatible with. Letting go is leaving an old job for one that comes with a salary increase. Going through your closet to discard clothes that no longer fit or shoes that are broken is also letting go.

It's not always a one-time event—letting go is often a process. You may let go of a job or relationship but carry their memories and residual impact with you for a time before you're able to fully detach from them. When we see the habit of letting go as a series of choices we slowly make until we no longer feel tied to what doesn't serve us, we're able to pinpoint our progress. Even if it's seven years down the line, putting another aspect of your past to rest *is* letting go.

INNER RESISTANCES TO LETTING GO

Whether it's a physical grip on sentimental clothes or an emotional grip on a relationship that's ended, many of us are resistant to the habit of letting go. Letting go is hard for a variety of reasons:

- **We are conditioned to hold on.** In childhood, we are taught never to give up, and that loving something means never letting it go. "Quitters never win" is a slogan posted in the locker rooms of tons of elementary and high school sporting facilities. "Hold on for dear life" is a popular phrase that makes it seem like letting go could mean the end of life as we know it. It's unsettling to let go of what we know, and no one wants to feel like a loser.

- **We are afraid of losing deep connection.** Maybe holding on keeps you connected in some way to a relationship you didn't want to end, a memory with a family member you don't want to forget, or a version of yourself you want to relive.

- **We are afraid of change.** Maybe holding on is rooted in fear and self-doubt. Perhaps holding on gives you a false sense of safety because it's familiar and you can remain on autopilot. Maybe you lack confidence in your ability to be successful after past failures. Change can feel scary and uncertain.

- **Letting go feels like failure.** Maybe your identity and worth are wrapped up in the things you've acquired, the roles you play in the lives of other people, and the things you do and achieve. Letting those things go, even if it's to start over, can feel like a failure.

- **Letting go means not getting a return on your investment.** Maybe you've spent years building a relationship or a large amount of money chasing a business idea, and now you're emotionally invested in ways that make it difficult to just walk away.

- **Letting go feels like punishment.** Maybe you were taught that admitting you are wrong is a form of chastisement. No one *wants* to be punished for making a mistake in judgment.

- **Some people think they can't move forward without closure.** Maybe you only know how to let go of things that have a clear end or an acceptable reason for ending.

We don't talk enough about the grief that comes with doing what's best for you. Things that are good *for* you don't always feel good *to* you, at first. Deciding to move forward, saying goodbye, and starting over can be a difficult process—but what's waiting for you on the other side is worth it.

It's also important to acknowledge that we are not always tasked with letting go of bad things. When I was growing up my grandmom would say, "Everything that's good to you ain't good for you." Of course, I had to mature enough to understand that piece of wisdom fully. But what she meant was that there are times in life when we must let go of things that may not be *bad* but may be a hindrance

> It is painful to let go of something you never wanted to end. To soothe the pain, we must remind ourselves that what we had is not the best we'll ever have. We let go to heal. We let go to make room for what's next.

to our greater good. This is one reason we might be reluctant to let go of friendships, goals, and projects that aren't fruitful, or beliefs about life that no longer align with who we are. Those things are not bad; they are just outgrown, and they may be blocking us from being as successful as we deserve.

In the most basic sense, holding on fulfills a need. We need to win, survive, be loved, and feel connected. Holding on to things, situations, and especially people fulfills our need for certainty and security, among other necessities. Those needs don't disappear just because what we use to fill them no longer works for us. We make it about the people and the things because they are easily identifiable, something we can easily grasp and hold on to. Truthfully, the issue is about *how* those people and things fulfill our needs.

I've evolved from saying "let go" to sometimes saying "release." When you release something, you set it free from confinement, allowing it to move, act, and flow as it pleases. It even sounds more positive—more poetic—when you say it out loud. *There are some things (or people) I need to release.*

WHY LETTING GO MATTERS

We let go to free ourselves from the emotional baggage that weighs us down and keeps us stuck in the past. We let go to give ourselves the physical and emotional space to welcome things that enhance our lives. We let go to build resilience and improve our mental health.

There are some things you need to let go of if you want to reach your full potential. When we normalize the habit of letting go of things that no longer align with who we are, we set ourselves free to experience the things that do. Letting go isn't about quitting, failing, or losing who you once were. Letting go is about doing what you have to do to meet your own needs—in healthier ways—so you can live a better life.

Though the process of letting go can be layered and complicated, *knowing* when to let go is simple. When you have to betray yourself to hold on, it's time to let go.

Some habits we hold on to and how they betray us

- **Replaying past scenarios in your head.** This habit is common for those who are looking for ways to re-create the outcome. By holding on to the story, you think you are controlling the narrative or adjusting the truth, but what you are doing is (a) reinjuring yourself emotionally, which causes more hurt, and (b) staying stuck in an unchangeable loop instead of freeing yourself up for other things. By choosing to let go, you give yourself closure.

- **Holding a grudge or seeking retribution.** Anger and frustration are inevitable emotions when it comes to a bad breakup, friendship betrayal, or lost professional opportunity. But hanging on to those feelings long after the event has passed isn't healthy for your mind, body, or spirit. Stubbornness or revenge don't move you forward. Choosing to process your experience, glean whatever lesson or wisdom you can from it, and give yourself permission to experience something better is the real flex.

- **Putting a temporary fix on a permanent problem.** When someone is resistant to letting go, they may try to fix something that is actually finished. This could range from a dead-end job to a broken relationship. Some people will suffer through financial deficit or even emotional neglect just to hold out hope for something they can't let go of. By being honest about your problem and surrendering your hold, you take back control of your life and clear a path for a replacement.

WHAT LETTING GO HEALS IN US

Sometime after my high school breakup, I was watching an episode of *The Oprah Winfrey Show* when I heard her say, "I won't let myself want anyone who doesn't want me." I said, *Amen!* out loud as if I was sitting in the first pew in church on Sunday. I repeated what Oprah said: *I won't let myself want anyone who doesn't want me*. With that small emotional release, I began a process of letting go.

Letting go breaks your attachment to anyone or anything that keeps you from moving forward with your life.

It is hard to accept that what you want doesn't want you back. But when you let go, relinquishing your attachment to things that are not in your best interest, you are sending a message to love, success, and goodness that you are open, ready, and worthy to receive what is.

Here is an exercise that will help you practice emotionally letting go. Take a moment here to reflect on the things you need to emotionally release and complete the prompt aloud or in your journal. You can take some time now to repeat this practice or come back to it later:

I won't let myself want _____ because I am worthy of

_____.

LETTING GO AND YOUR PURPOSE

Letting go of things that no longer serve us takes us one step closer to reclaiming our purpose. Once your sense of worthiness is restored, you are empowered to be hopeful about the future. Holding on keeps you chained to the past. Letting go gives you the freedom to focus on the things that are actually *for* you.

When your life is cluttered with hurtful memories, feelings of resentment or bitterness, or attachments that keep you stuck in old patterns of behavior, you are unable to distinguish between things that contribute to your purpose and things that threaten it.

I learned about something called psychological fortitude (PF)—which I had been calling emotional fortitude—from my friend Dr. Rheeda Walker. Our PF is our ability to take care of our daily needs. One of the biggest hindrances to doing that, and one of the biggest hindrances to becoming the best versions of ourselves (my definition of *purpose*), is distractions. When you release things that no longer serve you, you declutter the path of your life. *The habit of letting go keeps us from being distracted by the past.* You reclaim your purpose when you are focused on things that are in your best interest.

FOUR STEPS TO BEGIN
THE HEALTHY HABIT OF LETTING GO

Everything in life has an expiration date. As we move from one version of ourselves to the next, we must let go of things that may have supported, validated, and served us in the past, and embrace what represents who we want to be today. Begin the process of letting go by taking these steps:

1. **Exchange your negative emotions for healthier ones.** We've talked about the difficulty of letting go; now let's discuss how painful it can be to hold on. It is stressful, draining, and confusing to dwell in an unhappy relationship, job situation, or perpetual state of longing. Consider exchanging those emotions and others like exhaustion, anger, embarrassment, and regret for ease, contentment, admiration, and peace.

   Identify one act of letting go to engage in today. That act could be as simple as blocking someone on social media, starting a draft of your letter of resignation (you don't have to send it until you are in a position to do so), or starting the process of emptying a workspace. After identifying the act, name the feeling that letting go will inspire. Is it relief? Freedom? Excitement? A stronger sense of purpose?

2. **Examine your relationships and how they make you feel.** Cultivate a realistic view of the relationship so you are not hyper-focused on just the good. Stop over-romanticizing love. In real life, relationships end. Allow love and relationships to grow, evolve, and expire naturally. Just because it didn't last doesn't mean it was never meant to be. And what you lost is not the best you'll ever have. When you reflect on the truth of the relationship, you may see where you are no longer aligned or have outgrown each other, or how the version of yourself that you are today could benefit from a more supportive or thoughtful partner.

   Love when the opportunity presents itself, and let go when it's time—so a new opportunity can make its way into your life.

   When relationships end, it's helpful to journal your feelings. Process your thoughts and emotions instead of ruminating over them. Speaking (or writing) your thoughts often brings more peace into your life.

3. **Dream of reinventing yourself: Who do you see?** Embrace a new skill, talent, or hobby. Immerse yourself in self-discovery. Invite things that align with the new version of yourself. Take an art, dance, or cooking class. Join a book club or community organization. Eventually you will see that by letting go, you are gaining—not losing.

   Make a list of accomplishments and add to them. Letting go doesn't mean you have to leave everything behind. What have you done well? How can you do more of what you are good at?

   Engage in mindfulness practices. Stay present through prayer, meditation, and deep breathing.

4. **Give yourself the closure you need to continue moving forward.** Closure will look different for everyone, but it's a universal part of the process of letting go. Decide what closure looks and feels like for you. You might consider performing a ritual. Some people write letters that they burn or throw away. If you are letting go of a relationship, you might choose to have a final conversation that lets the person know exactly how you feel.

What has worked for me is to assign meaning to the experience, knowing that it contributes to my desire to reclaim my purpose. If someone was a good friend to me and we had fun, traveled together, and built memories, I resign it to that season in my life—understanding that seasons change.

What meaning can you assign to the thing you are letting go of? What good memories does it hold? What did you learn or gain from it? Once you uncover the meaning, let it rest.

PROMPTS FOR LETTING GO

What/who do you need to let go of or release? Consider your relationships, environment, and things from your past. What are you holding on to that no longer serves you? Are you trying to relive something from your past? Are there some things in your life that are not good for your mental and emotional health?

Why do you need to let go? Knowing why will help you focus on the need and not the person or thing that meets or no longer meets the need. Why won't you throw broken things away? Why is it hard to let go of the relationship? How will letting go change your life?

What does letting go look like for you? What are some items in

your home, car, or office that you need to stop hoarding? Are there
any broken or unused items that once meant something to you but
don't align with the person you are becoming?

*How will you practice the habit of letting go today, this week, and/or
this month? What are the actions you can commit to doing?* Commit to
focusing on your new story and supporting this version of yourself. Create a lifestyle of releasing anything or anyone that no longer meets your needs. Will you remove some people from your
contact list? Will you declutter a closet in your home or clean out
your garage this week?

**You are doing the work to reclaim your purpose by letting go.
I want you to read through the following out loud with me if
you can. Whatever comes to mind as you read through, let this
be your sign confirming that it is time to let go.**

When you question its place in your life . . .
When it takes away more than it adds . . .
When just the thought of letting go gives you a feeling of
    relief . . .
When it's clear that it no longer wants you . . .
When it stands in the way of your progress . . .
When it depletes you of your good energy . . .
When it steals your peace . . .
When it steals your joy . . .
When it makes you forget who you are . . .
When it blocks your blessings . . .

Let it go.

USE THE SPACE BELOW TO WORK
THROUGH THE PROMPTS ON YOUR OWN

Need: _____

_____

_____

Why do I need to do this? _____

_____

_____

Healing Habits: _____

_____

_____

Practices/Action: _____

_____

_____

AFFIRMATIONS FOR LETTING GO

Say this out loud with me:

I reclaim all of my energy from the past.
I honor this version of myself with my whole heart.
I release everything and everyone that has already
   released me.
I am open to better.
I choose people and things that choose me.

Chapter 3

THE HABIT OF PLAYING YOUR ROLE: HOW PERSONAL ACCOUNTABILITY HEALS OUR RELATIONSHIP WITH CONTROL

I am not perfect. No one is. So when you make a mistake, _just admit it and allow yourself to grow from it._

I shared those words with my son after he broke the latest computer screen his father had just purchased for him. He is known for breaking things. For several years in a row, because of that reputation, we did not give him any new gadgets, including the PS5 he was wishing for. He is not the kind of guy who likes to _cause_ trouble; he just somehow found himself in the vicinity of trouble—every week. You know the type.

Still, this year was one of growth for him. I watched as slowly but surely, his attitude started to shift. He was more intentional with the things he carried and tried to take better care of what was already in his possession. The shift began a few months earlier when I introduced him to the concept of impact versus intention—a lesson I had learned the hard way, the day that my dad gave me a hundred dollars to hold for him before the start of one of his baseball games.

Before he went down to the dugout, I asked my dad if I could use some of the money to buy my usual snack of chips and a soda. "Yes, but that's it," he said, before running down to start the game. I had to have been young—definitely under nine. And there I was . . . standing in front of the concession stand with a pocketful of money. A few of my friends came over and *needed* snacks, so of course I had to hook them up. Then a few of their friends came over and needed snacks too, so I hooked them up. In the moment, I felt like the coolest kid there. And before I knew it, my pocket wasn't as full anymore. But, hey . . . at least my friends and I had a time, right?

After playing a long game, my dad was starving. We stopped at McDonald's to get some food, and he asked for the money he'd given me. I dug in my pockets and gave him what little I had left. As you can imagine, that didn't go over well. Let's just say the ball wasn't the only thing my dad hit that night.

I turned and looked at my son. "I didn't mean to spend so much money," I explained. "I only wanted to share what I had with my friends. But sometimes even the best intentions can have a negative impact on others." As it turns out, most of the money my dad had asked me to hold was supposed to go to my grandmom so she could pay the phone bill. That was my first lesson in personal accountability.

I could see my son internalizing the lesson as he tilted his head and began to nod up and down in agreement. "Intention versus impact. I get it. But, Mom, spending a hundred dollars on junk food for your friends is crazy! Even I know not to do that." (Says the guy with the reputation . . .)

There are times when we have a specific idea or plan that negatively impacts someone or something else—even when it was well-intended. We make mistakes that have a lasting financial, physical, or emotional impact on others. There are times when our actions are meant to help and support, but they end up causing harm. No matter the situation, it is important that we accept responsibility and take accountability, even when the intention doesn't match the outcome.

PERSONAL ACCOUNTABILITY
GOES BOTH WAYS

Angel was thirteen years old, and his family's case had been as-signed to me by a judge. After a period of intense misbehavior by Angel, his father decided he had done all he could for the boy and walked into his local police precinct, intending to drop him off. Of course, the officers asked for more information. What danger did the young boy pose? What laws had he broken? The father couldn't think of any broken laws, but he described many instances where Angel didn't come straight home after school, stayed out past cur-few, talked back to him, and even hit him back during a whup-ping. The father and son were referred to family court, which eventually referred them to me.

Angel's father was a first-generation Dominican American who worked hard to build a successful contracting business and pro-vide for his family. He was an older man, whose strict views on parenting often collided with the views of his American-born teenage son. By the time I started working with the family, Angel had run away from home several times.

My job was to assess the family's needs, determine what refer-rals and resources to provide, create a case plan, and monitor the family's progress through counseling and training sessions. I de-cided to meet with Angel first so I could have an objective view of the boy who had overwhelmed his father so much that he thought he could walk into a police station, tell his story, and walk out without Angel.

Angel had a big physical presence—not many thirteen-year-olds are pushing six feet—but he was still unassuming. After he walked in with his head down, greeted me with a soft "hey," and I started asking him questions, I was surprised at how respectful and self-aware he was.

Here's what I learned from my session with Angel:

- His father worked between twelve and sixteen hours a day and expected Angel to look out for his mother and siblings during that time.

- Angel couldn't play sports or hang out with friends because of his responsibilities at home.

- His father was a recovering alcoholic who used to scare the family when he was drunk. Things would often get physical.

- Angel resented his father for the years of alcoholism, his own lack of a social life, and for not being open to understanding his generation/culture.

My session with Angel's father was brief and to the point. He walked into the conference room with paint and dirt all over his work clothes and boots, greeting me with a look of frustration and defeat.

Here's what I learned from my session with Angel's father:

- Angel was the oldest of the four children he'd had with his second (and current) wife.

- He had four adult children from his first marriage and hadn't planned to start all over again, years later.

- He started working with his own father when he was nine years old and never finished school.

- He saw Angel as ungrateful and disrespectful, especially since the boy was a main reason why the father had to continue working so hard at his age.

Angel and his father blamed each other for their difficulty. Both of them felt they had a legitimate right to behave the way they did, but that defensiveness also led Angel and his father to neglect each of their personal responsibilities in their relationship. On each side, there was a clear lack of accountability for that neglect—something they would come to learn goes both ways.

RESPONSIBILITY SETS US UP FOR ACCOUNTABILITY

People aren't always aware that they are dodging their personal responsibilities. So when an unexpected unpleasant consequence arises—tension within a relationship, estrangement, or retaliatory responses from others—they can't see how they've contributed to it, since that's not how they intended for things to turn out. Sometimes our intentions keep us from seeing the part we play in our own struggle. But a lack of awareness of your responsibility doesn't mean you aren't still accountable for it.

Dealing with someone who doesn't accept responsibility for their actions can be frustrating. Their lack of accountability can overwhelm you. They are manipulative, which is draining. They will bully, argue, revise the truth, avoid, and retreat altogether until they think you've forgotten what they've done.

My goal for Angel was to invite him to see that although his father was one hundred percent responsible for his foul behavior as an alcoholic, his lack of consideration of Angel's life, and for punishing him physically, *Angel* was one hundred percent accountable for his own actions. He would ultimately be the one to endure the consequences of breaking the rules of his father's home, not giving his full effort at school, and responding to violence with violence.

Signs that someone lacks the ability to accept personal accountability

• *They consistently blame others for their current circumstances.* A slow driver, traffic, or an alarm not waking them up is the reason they're late—not their poor planning and time management.

• *They play the role of victim long after the offense has happened,* citing that experience as the eternal cause of every experience that follows. They experienced bullying as a child, and that's the reason they have low self-esteem, can't get along with others, have trouble with co-workers, and don't have any friends as an adult. This person may not start drama, but they always seem to align themselves with it, just to prove they are right that "everyone always gives me a hard time."

• *They downplay their contribution to negative outcomes.* They start arguments and say the other person is overreacting. They may leave out important details from the story of what happened. They use phrases like "all I said was," "all I did was," or consistently hide behind "I didn't know"—when the full truth is that they were an instigator, they were passive-aggressive, or they violated a boundary and can't handle the consequence.

My goal for Angel's father was to invite him to see that some of the stressors he was experiencing were created by the habits he had learned to survive in the past. His recent work in recovery was admirable, but it didn't erase the impact of his prior abuse. It was also important for Angel's father to acknowledge that he was treating Angel like an ungrateful and disrespectful child, while at the same time giving him the responsibilities of a full-grown adult. That kind of dynamic is difficult for a child to manage.

During Angel's father's first session, I asked him to look back on his own childhood—how he was forced to work instead of attending school, and how he was denied the opportunity to choose his own path in life. "When you look back," I asked, "do you see a happy child?"

> If others have described you in some of the ways we discuss in this chapter, take a deep breath in and exhale. You wouldn't be reading this book if you didn't want to release negative habits. Maybe your negative habit is avoiding personal responsibility. That's okay. Just remember you are here to gain awareness of habits that will help you heal and become the person you are meant to be.

Normally a man of many words, ready to defend himself or reject accusations, Angel's father paused. I could see him holding space for the younger version of himself. The father in him was experiencing empathy for his son—having once lived in the same shoes. He broke down in tears before he could even answer the question.

Over the next six months, Angel and his father began to mend their relationship. They attended family therapy and anger management sessions. The parents found childcare for the younger children, and Angel started playing football. Angel worked for his father on Saturday mornings and remarked that he would *think* about taking over the business one day but wouldn't make any promises. Things weren't perfect, but when they made compromises and also worked on taking responsibility for their personal roles in the family, Angel finally felt heard and his father felt less overwhelmed.

DEFINING PERSONAL ACCOUNTABILITY

Angel and his father did two things to contribute to healing their family. They accepted *responsibility* for their own actions and were willing to be *accountable* for making the changes that would benefit the entire family. We often use these words interchangeably, but there is a difference between responsibility and accountability, and both are needed to create new and healthy habits.

A responsibility is something that is your job or duty to deal with. Maybe your actions caused a particular outcome. You broke a computer screen or crossed a boundary in your relationship. Or perhaps you are responsible because you are a person in authority, and one of your direct reports is creating a hostile environment in your workplace. In either case, your role in the situation is what puts responsibility on your shoulders.

Accountability is a willingness to accept responsibility. Accountability is responsibility in action. This might look like extending an apology, changing your behavior, or making amends. A person who is accountable says, "I caused the outcome," even if it wasn't their intention. "I accept the consequences and will work to remedy it."

Holding yourself accountable doesn't always mean you were the responsible party or the one who caused the outcome. It means that, in an effort to move forward, you're taking on the duty of handling things because you're invested in contributing to a favorable outcome.

Taking responsibility for your actions can be as simple as acknowledging them. *Yes, I did it, I said it, I broke it, I made a mistake.* Accountability requires that some sort of action be taken in addition to the acknowledgment.

We tend to equate personal accountability with blame, fault, liability, or moral obligation, but it is so much more than that. By taking accountability, even if we had good intentions or we're choosing to be accountable for the impact someone else caused, we are empowered to be catalysts for change. There is no shame in accountability.

> *Accountability looks like*
> * *Extending an apology*
> * *Correcting a mistake*
> * *Changing a specific behavior that has negatively impacted your life or someone else's*
> * *Showing actionable empathy to someone impacted by your actions ("I understand how my actions inconvenienced you, so I will give you space to recover")*
> * *Validating/holding space for someone's feelings about a situation you caused ("I can see how that was hurtful, and I take responsibility for my role in it")*

OUR RESISTANCE TO PERSONAL ACCOUNTABILITY

I had a bad attitude, I'll be the second to admit. The first person to bring it to my attention was Eric, my friend from college.

One day we were sitting outside the Canteen, and I was drinking a Mango Mystic when he said, "Nobody likes you." I was shocked! *Nobody likes me?! Really?!* I was being sarcastic—something Eric would have to get used to if we were going to remain friends. I assumed nobody liked me because *I* liked nobody. At that point, I was over people. I had just broken up with my childhood sweetheart and several friendships had recently ended in betrayal. I told myself I was too busy to form new relationships, but really I was busy building up my walls, making sure I didn't get hurt again.

My behavior reflected all of that. I turned down invitations to hang out and sat far away from everyone in class. If someone said something I didn't like, or looked at me the wrong way, I would snap back defensively. I didn't like to fight, but when it came to verbal aggression, I was known to attack.

Eric said, "You're not a mean person at heart, I can tell." He told me to lighten up and take down the wall I'd been putting up with people. I could feel his genuine concern—he wanted other people to experience me in the way he had.

Eric asked me why I behaved one way in class or around other people, and a whole other way when it was just me and him. He was truly curious and waited for an answer. I rolled my eyes because I had no good explanation, or at least not one he would understand. I was from Jersey, from the hood. I felt like I had a right to behave the way I did after all I'd been through and survived. I had already told Eric about my broken relationships and shared a few stories about life in the projects. Clearly, he didn't see any of that as an excuse for my behavior. He told me I was turning people away for no reason and assigned himself the job of bringing it to my attention whenever he noticed.

Over the next school year, he called me out every chance he could. (And with an attitude like mine, he had many, many chances.) If I was using a defensive or aggressive tone, he would cut me off mid-sentence and ask me to "tone it down" and try again. When I rolled my eyes at something, he asked me why I was doing that—with a genuine interest in holding space for my feelings and allowing me to practice more mature responses. He also showed empathy for my experiences, validating my need to be protective of myself, while also inviting me to be accountable for where I was now. Eric saw me sabotaging the possibility of healthy connections, and he was right.

I was resistant to taking accountability for my actions because I thought I had a right to act out. My habitual bad attitude was a direct result of being wronged by others, and I had kept that attitude for protection. But now I was making people I didn't know pay for things people they didn't know had done to me. In consequence, the person who paid most dearly for my negative habits was me. I told myself that I didn't care if people liked me, but that wasn't true. I cared deeply.

> **Things to keep in mind**
>
> * *Your past trauma is not an excuse for you to act messy or petty.*
> * *Just because someone doesn't accept responsibility for their actions doesn't mean they won't experience the consequences of them.*
> * *Your goal should not be to get back at the people who hurt you.*
> * *No one will feel the impact of your bad habits more than you. Hurt people don't always hurt people. Some of us heal, grow, and live our lives helping others do the same.*

Hard truth: Sometimes it's you. Sometimes you are the cause, the reason for your own struggle. Much of the work of self-healing involves working through things someone else has done to us in the past, but we don't talk enough about how our unwillingness to own our stuff can prevent us from truly doing the work to heal. If you look only outside of yourself, you will be blind to the power you have on the inside of you to transform your own life.

If you are the cause, you are the cure.

If you are the problem, you are the solution.

If you made the wrong choice, you can make the right one next time.

Anything that you do, you have the power to undo—or do better.

WHY PERSONAL ACCOUNTABILITY MATTERS

It gives you ownership. When you own something, you inherit rights. As with a car, house, or even clothes you've purchased, owning gives you the right to make changes or upgrades based on your needs. That is what taking personal accountability does for you. Owning your part gives you the right to change your mind, and pivot when things are no longer working. Ownership is saying "I caused it" or "I acknowledge it" and "I am willing to do my part to change."

You take ownership of your life when you acknowledge

- How being the person who is always late affects other people's time

- How "just being honest" can come across as harsh to someone who is sensitive

- How something you didn't intend to do as a friend, parent, partner, or neighbor still caused harm to someone you love

It gives you influence. When you control something, you gain power and influence. Taking accountability for the things you didn't cause gives you the power to determine what happens next. You are not to blame for the consequences your parents' alcoholism, emotional unavailability, or poor financial habits caused, but you might be the only one who can break that negative cycle and mitigate the impact it still has on your life. Choosing healthy ways of coping and moving forward is a power move.

You take control of your own life every time you refuse to do to others what has been done to you. Instead of matching the energy of others, you decide to show empathy, think independently, and show up as a healed version of yourself. When you go to therapy, practice prayer and meditation, develop healthy habits, and cultivate healthy relationships—you create your own path in life.

It gives you hope. Taking ownership of your life gives you the promise of something better. With so many uncontrollable aspects of life, personal accountability gives you a tangible way to remain hopeful that your outcomes will be favorable. With accountability, there is an assurance that with effort, you can recover from a mistake, find closure in relationships, and see new opportunities in other areas of your life.

WHAT PERSONAL ACCOUNTABILITY HEALS IN US

When you choose not to accept personal accountability, you give your power over to whomever (or whatever) you're choosing to blame. If everyone else is responsible for the things that go wrong in your life, who gets the credit when things go right? Either someone else has the power or you do. You can't just transfer that power when it's convenient.

I made a lot of personal changes during that first year of college. I wouldn't say I became a social butterfly, but I made friends that I am still connected to today. I smiled more when in public (which is totally off-brand for a Jersey girl). I took responsibility for my behavior and held myself accountable for the impact my attitude had on others.

I also had to face some painful truths about some of the people I allowed into my life. We are accountable not only for how we show up in the lives of others, but for how we allow others to show up in our lives. You can't control a single soul outside of yourself, but you can choose friends who are consistent, well-meaning, and reciprocal. You can choose partners who don't put you down and who are not abusive. You can set boundaries or distance yourself from family members who make you uncomfortable or have caused you harm in the past. A part of being accountable is doing your part to protect yourself when you have the power to do so.

Here are healthier ways of protecting yourself

- *Believe what you see a person do, not just what they say.*
- *Be open to new relationships with people whose intentions are pure.*
- *Speak up for yourself in a way that is assertive, not aggressive, when you've been wronged.*
- *Leave behind the need for vengeance or getting even.*
- *Advocate for yourself in your relationships, on the job, and when you are at risk.*

I want to acknowledge that some horrific, unimaginable, and undeserved things happen to us at the hands of others. As children, we were at the mercy of the adults charged with the responsibility to care for us, and some of those adults did horrible jobs. Those situations were outside of our control. If that's your family history, hear this from me: You didn't cause it. You didn't deserve it. You are not responsible for that. Your single duty during that time in your life was to survive. Well done.

It can be tempting to seek retribution. It can be tempting to prove your power through aggressive and retaliatory behavior. No one wants to experience any more layers of pain, but you don't have to do to others what was done to you. You don't have to hurt people before they hurt you. You don't have to punish the people who want to love you now for what the people who didn't know how to love you in the past did to your heart.

PERSONAL ACCOUNTABILITY AND RECLAIMING OUR PURPOSE

So far the path to reclaiming our purpose has led us to identify our personal best through self-care and stay focused on our best interests by letting go. Personal accountability empowers us to self-correct and regain control of our lives when someone or something else takes us off course.

Personal accountability keeps us in the driver's seat of our lives. Anything I do, I can undo. Anything I learn, I can unlearn. Anything I cause, I can cure. The more we lean into habits that give us control over our relationships, careers, and ourselves, the more our behavior will be healthier, stronger, and better aligned with our purpose.

Instead of seeing accountability as a punishment for making a mistake or a chore assigned to you because of someone else's mistake, see it as an opportunity to reinvent yourself as many times as it takes to become the person you are meant to be.

THREE MORE STEPS TO BEGIN THE HABIT OF PERSONAL ACCOUNTABILITY

1. **You may have to heal from things no one ever apologized for.** You may never receive an apology from your parents about your childhood, from your spouse for violating your relationship, from your friend for ghosting you or your boss for firing you. You have a responsibility to yourself to heal anyway.

2. **You may have to be the one to end a relationship that is unhealthy for you.** Some marriages, partnerships, and

friendships last far longer than the actual relationship because neither party is willing to accept responsibility for protecting their own heart. Have the tough conversations about your needs and standards up-front to see if the person you are in a relationship with is open to change. If they choose to continue engaging in unhealthy patterns, choose yourself and move forward without them.

3. **You may have to admit you were wrong or made a mistake.** Our choices have a direct impact on the lives around us, and it takes courage to acknowledge if a choice we made was harmful. When you do this, you are standing as the highest version of yourself and giving others the opportunity to witness your true character. Let others see that you have integrity, you know how to self-correct, you care about how your actions impact others, and that you are committed to being a better person.

We've unpacked a lot of things about cultivating the habit of accepting personal accountability. Now let's take some time to reflect on ways you can put this habit into practice.

PROMPTS FOR PERSONAL ACCOUNTABILITY

What do you need to take personal accountability for in your life? Have your actions caused harm in the life of someone you love? Have someone else's actions toward you led to behavior that you are not proud of? Do you need to speak up for yourself more? Do you need to release your excuses and stop using your past to stay in a victim cycle?

Why do you need to be more accountable in those areas? Knowing your why will help you focus on the outcome, not the possible shame or regret of waiting so long.

What does being more accountable for your life look like? What can you do to meet your own needs and protect your own heart, and in what ways do you need to be more accountable for how you show up in the lives of others? Will you have more tough conversations, set boundaries, or release some people from your life?

How will you practice the habit of accepting personal accountability today, this week, and/or this month? What are the actions you can commit to doing? What can you do immediately? Can you examine the impact your actions have had on others and change your behavior moving forward? Can you initiate a tough conversation about how someone else's actions have impacted you?

Practicing the habit of accepting personal accountability will require trying behaviors you are not used to. Protecting yourself by initiating a conversation with someone who hurt you may feel intimidating, or you may even feel resentful that you have to initiate that conversation in the first place. You may feel weak for admitting that your action negatively impacted someone you love or feel foolish for having to publicly correct a mistake. Remember your why, and stay committed to your healing.

USE THE SPACE BELOW TO WORK
THROUGH THE PROMPTS ON YOUR OWN

Need: _____

_____

_____

Why do I need to do this? _____

_____

_____

Healing Habits: _____

_____

_____

Practices/Action: _____

_____

_____

AFFIRMATIONS FOR PERSONAL ACCOUNTABILITY

Say this out loud with me:

I accept full responsibility for my life.
Taking accountability for my life empowers me.
I am capable of recovering from every mistake.
I am committed to becoming the best version of myself.
I will give myself space to learn and grow.

PART TWO

RECLAIM YOUR PEACE

Sorrow prepares you for joy. It violently
sweeps everything out of your house, so
that new joy can find space to enter.

—RUMI

Chapter 4

THE HABIT OF LOWERING EXPECTANCE HEALS OUR RELATIONSHIP WITH BITTERNESS

Some major life changes happened for me when I was ten years old. I got braces and glasses, and I started attending a private Christian school thanks to a payment plan for low-income families. Here's the thing: I didn't like any of it. First, it was the new school. Switching schools is tough for anyone, and I was a Black girl from the projects whose parents were the same age as some of my classmates' older siblings. And I didn't even live with my parents, so in class I always ended up correcting teachers who said things like, "Take this home to your mother," or "What did your mother think about that?"

The week leading up to Mother's Day was particularly awful. One teacher brought in construction paper in assorted colors, markers, glitter, crayons, stickers, and glue. She raved about the Mother's Day creations she had made when she was a kid and encouraged us to be creative in our expressions of love and gratitude for our moms. Initially, I was excited to get started. But things took a turn as my teachers and the other students noticed that I was making two cards. All day I had to explain that I needed something for both my grandmom (whom I called Mom at the time) and my *actual* mom (whom I also called Mom). My teachers kept pushing back against my two cards. "We're celebrating mothers, Nakeia. We'll have something special for grandparents on Grandparents' Day."

I felt so different from everyone else at school. There were only two Black students in our entire grade level, and I was the only one who didn't come from a so-called traditional family. My skin color was different, my background was different, the community I bused in from was different, and my experiences up to that point were something none of my classmates could relate to. I lived in the hood, and my family didn't have money—the students loved to make fun of the old yellow Ford that we drove. To top it all off, one Monday morning, I showed up at school with braces *and* glasses. Luckily, a few weeks later, those glasses "disappeared" under mysterious circumstances (and my grandmom didn't have the money to replace them). As for the braces, I was stuck with those for five whole years. These are not the worst things that can happen to a kid, but it sure feels like it when you're ten years old.

Before changing schools, I had no idea that the story of my life was so . . . *layered*. At my old school, it was common for kids to live with their grandmothers, and tons of my friends were born to teenage parents. Not to mention, the kids I knew who didn't *come from the projects* still liked to hang out there, so I hadn't yet realized it was a rough place to grow up. All of us were united by a struggle we were too young to understand.

When my new classmates shared the details of their lives, it opened my eyes to ways of being that I didn't even know were possible. Parents could be married and live together, happily. Adults could earn enough money from a single job to support their families. There were no fights after school, I didn't have to prove I was tough, and I saw kids experiencing the luxury of just being kids. Life outside of struggle existed.

After school, I would come home and pray, *God, what's up with my life? Why the struggle? Why no real family? Why the major differences in the quality of life between the Black people I live around and the white people I go to school with?*

Although I felt different, I didn't feel less than anyone else. I still knew I had a right to a quality education—and, ultimately, a higher-quality life—despite all the things that made me different. In fact, having a layered story made me feel significant. That's one thing I will always appreciate about myself—I never hid any part of my story. I didn't shy away from the uncomfortable details. When everyone else was making Mother's Day cards, I continued to make two—one for each of the women I called "Mom."

When you're ready to start practicing the habit of acceptance, making peace with your childhood is a good place to start. We don't get to choose our foundation; it is what it is. And you know what, when those foundational experiences sucked, there's a chance that a good portion of our adult lives might suck as well. But one day, someone like me might come along and invite you to accept what sucked. The audacity!

Stick close, Beloved. I'm going somewhere with this.

ACCEPTING THINGS YOU DIDN'T CHOOSE

When each of us was born, we didn't get to stand behind a one-way mirror and pick our parents out of a lineup. The first time we met them was the same moment we took our very first breaths. Some people win the parent lottery, others just learn to live with what they get.

It's important to have a bit of grace for everyone here. Some of our parents had to navigate their roles under horrible circumstances. They did what they could—when they could. Others of us might have been affected by things beyond the actions of our parental figures—for example, how our environment, extended family, community, country, nationality, or color has impacted us.

I once had a client whose entire community raised money and collected resources for her to move to the United States to attend college in New York. She was a standout in her medical residency, living out her family's wishes and "the American dream." Yet she still felt extremely unfulfilled, and even a little angry. She was a textbook people-pleaser who didn't understand why it was so hard for her to *feel* happy—until she realized she was living someone else's dream. In her culture, it was common for the family and community elders to decide early on the kind of life young people were to live. She had been a doctor in training her whole life. In our work together, we identified her core values and explored what made her feel fully present and aligned with her desires. Eventually, she uncovered that what she really wanted to do was write.

There are so many things from childhood that we don't get to choose

- *Who our parents are*
- *The quality of parenting we receive (present parents, absent parents, and their maturity levels)*
- *How we are raised (culture, values, spiritual beliefs)*
- *Being a minority*
- *Growing up in an impoverished community*
- *Experiencing abuse or neglect of any kind*

It was difficult for my client to name her habit of people-pleasing and self-abandonment because it was ingrained in her culture to do so. Once the veil was lifted, she realized it was never really her choice. It was hard for her to accept that even as an adult, she wasn't fully in control of her own life.

DEFINING ACCEPTANCE

I used to strongly dislike that phrase: *It is what it is*. Somewhere on social media, I saw someone call it a toxic phrase, and at first that characterization resonated with me. It seemed like people used it only when they were giving up on something or making an excuse for not living up to a promise.

"Hey, are you going to try again?" *No. It is what it is.*

"You don't even appear to be sorry." *Well, it is what it is.*

"You are always late and it's frustrating." *I'm sorry, but it is what it is.*

If someone uses the phrase to excuse their lack of personal responsibility, dismiss someone else's experience or feelings, or exercise their unwillingness to change, that can feel toxic. But I want to challenge you to consider a healthier way to use the phrase: as a reminder not to resist reality or force things that we can't change.

"No, I don't want to continue this relationship with you." *Okay. It is what it is.*

"Can we try to make things work one more time?" *No. It is what it is.*

> When I say it is what it is I mean
>
> * I acknowledge what's happening in my life right now.
> * I choose not to resist reality.
> * I will not try to force what can't be.
> * I acknowledge the things I can't change.
> * I am aware that there are things I can't control.

"Don't you wish things were different?" *Yes. But it is what it is.*

All of us face moments when we need to close a chapter in our lives, acknowledge a truth about our story, or protect our own peace. When we reach that point, the habit of acceptance—or making peace with what is—can be a powerful practice in moving forward. Keep in mind: It is what it is right now, but one day it will be what you make it.

OUR RESISTANCE TO ACCEPTANCE

There are many ways we have developed a resistance to acceptance. A layered childhood isn't limited to kids of teenage parents, or the impoverished or abused. Just because you grew up in a traditional home doesn't mean you were shielded from struggle.

Perhaps you experienced emotional neglect from a parent who worked constantly or was too busy fussing over one of your siblings to be available to you. Maybe your guardian was overbearing and you felt like you couldn't do anything right. Or what if you grew up in an entirely wonderful home, but you were bullied at school?

If you are struggling to practice acceptance of your past, now is a good time to revisit your inner child. Hold space for the impact your life has had on you, and look at how far you've come despite it all.

Make space now for the little one in you to see that your past was temporary. It was what it was. And although those difficult moments were uncomfortable and painful, you eventually gained control of your own life.

Yes—you are a fighter, but this time you are fighting *for* your life, not against it. You are taking care of yourself, letting the past go, holding yourself accountable for your current behavior, and embracing acceptance.

DAILY HABITS TO HEAL RESISTANCE AND PRACTICE ACCEPTANCE

Stop trying to revise the past and start making active plans for how you want to live now and in the future.

Every morning I engage in a routine that I call *the Daily Setup*. I sit down and make a bulleted list of three to six things I'm planning to do that day. As I complete each bullet point, I highlight the item in my favorite color marker. Yes—seeing pink throughout the pages of my calendar makes me feel satisfied, but it is also a written reminder of my recent life accomplishments. I don't just make a daily plan, I make plans for the year, every quarter, every month, and every week. Planning your future sends a clear message that you will not be defined by your past.

Stop living someone else's dream. Be an original thinker, with ideas and beliefs that are aligned with who you are.

It's okay to be different. You can allow your family members to honor the traditions and values they hold as truth, while actively creating and uncovering your own. With this practice, simply allow others to be who they are while honoring who you are becoming each day.

Stop fighting things you can't change and start focusing on leveraging the gifts, skills, and talents you can use to transform your life.

Distract yourself with yourself. This practice keeps your attention directed toward things you can control. A healthy distraction could look like taking a class, developing a course of your own, or going after a promotion at work. You may not have been able to start off your life the way you wish you could have, but you can start fresh, right now.

WHY ACCEPTANCE MATTERS

Practicing acceptance can be as layered as the details of our lives. There are some things that we may have to accept for a season. There are circumstances we have to tolerate until we can regain control of our lives, or gain the resources and opportunities to do something else. Circumstances like your job, living situation, rela-

tionship status, and family dynamics all qualify as things you may
have to accept temporarily.

Acceptance is a major key to the happiness so many of us are
seeking. Happiness is about joy and contentment, and those
things won't flourish if we don't find peace. When you can't immediately change your circumstances, it's possible to find moments of joy even in temporary situations.

In my work I often get asked about situations like this:

*My parents make living at home unbearable. They are verbally
abusive and toxic. What can I do until I can move out?*

My response: Find something that you can do outside the
home that will take up as much of your day as possible and
bring moments of relief. Try a job you enjoy, join a small group,
or cultivate a new skill.

*My goal to buy a home keeps getting pushed back because I can't
seem to pay down my debt and save enough money. I feel like a
loser and it's making me depressed. Any tips?*

My response: Adjust your timeline. It's your goal, so you get to
make the rules. Instead of resisting the reality of your life right
now, work within it. Create a three- or five-year plan and celebrate every dollar you save and every debt you pay off. And this
is important: Make your current home as beautiful as possible.
Show gratitude, decorate it to fit the energy you want to live in,
and don't put off enjoying life "until . . ."

I want you to think of acceptance as releasing your desire for
something to be what it is not. Your parents can only be who they
are. Your past can only be what it was. The world you live in can
only be what it is—at least right now.

Acceptance isn't just *it is what it is*; acceptance is *it is what it is, right now.* Accepting what is right now doesn't disqualify you from experiencing what you desire in the future. It's also not the same thing as settling. I am not inviting you to engage in passive resignation, nor do I want you to give up. And don't tolerate unpalatable situations or things that you could change if you really wanted to. Acceptance is about what is *and* what will be. Your future is still unfolding.

WHAT ACCEPTANCE HEALS IN US

My dad walked up to me at my wedding reception with tears in his eyes. But this wasn't the sweet father-daughter moment you might be imagining. Our relationship wasn't that. My dad wasn't wearing a tux. He had on one of his famous matching joggers and hoodie sets and was carrying a big white shopping bag that I eventually opened to find a large ceramic angel with a broken wing, wrapped in swaths of tissue paper.

> *Other ways to define acceptance*
>
> - *Acceptance is the acknowledgment that things, people, or the past won't be any different than they already are.*
> - *Acceptance is acknowledging reality without judgment.*
> - *Acceptance is choosing not to resist what is.*
> - *Acceptance is embracing experiences for what they are.*
> - *Acceptance is releasing negative emotions about things outside of your control.*

I hadn't seen my dad in months, but I did talk with him when he called from prison, about a week earlier. He was calling to tell me he would be home to walk me down the aisle. I didn't get my hopes up. I didn't want to be disappointed. So I just said, "Okay," and hung up the call.

The next time I saw him, he was walking up to me at the reception. He wasn't at the rehearsal or rehearsal dinner, and he wasn't there for the ceremony either. But here he was, hours after I said "I do."

I had seen my dad cry only one other time in my entire life, when we had a tough conversation about his drug use. So in that moment at my reception, I just hugged him, said thanks for the gift, and whispered in his ear, "I'm not mad and I love you."

For years, I resented my father. For years, I wrestled with missing and needing the old daddy I knew and loved, instead of the new version who struggled with addiction and couldn't show up for me. As an adult, I grew to realize that even though his best didn't always feel good, he was doing the best he could. Still, for much of my childhood, his actions had left me feeling hurt, abandoned, and insecure. That part of my story didn't go away just because I'd chosen to accept him for who he was.

I promised myself after that last call from prison that I would let go of my hope for a resurgence of my old dad and accept and love the one I had now. I knew he loved me in his own way. He showed up for me when he could. When I said I wasn't mad and that I loved him, I meant it.

The practices that got me to this point in my relationship with my dad didn't just happen overnight. After years of harboring resentment, I slowly began to practice the habit of acceptance, and eventually I was able to choose forgiveness.

Sometimes people aren't intentionally letting us down. Sometimes we set them up to fail us by expecting them to play a role that they don't have the tools to play. This can happen in all kinds of relationships. It happens on the job among team members, it happens in intimate partner relationships, and it happens among friends. Lowering your expectations doesn't mean lowering your standards. We have to get real about what someone can bring to the relationship.

Over time, I accepted my dad for who he was and let go of what I wished he could be. This was a painful process. I had to hold a lot of space for the little girl in me who just wanted her daddy. I grieved for the loss of the man I once knew. And then I started accepting the dad who still wanted to pray for me, find out how his grandchildren were doing in school, and sing "Happy Birthday" on my answering machine every year. Giving others the freedom to be themselves makes room for authentic connection.

For some people, acceptance means letting go of the relationship altogether. When someone's capacity is a threat to your mental and emotional health, it may be in your best interest to keep your distance. There were times when I went years without communicating with my father because it was just too painful and draining to continue engaging with him. Our proximity had started to create bitterness in my heart toward him.

Bitterness is deeper than a flash of emotion in the moment. It's something you take with you, long after the moment or event has passed, that sits heavily on your heart. Bitterness might even seep into your behavior, making you cynical, hostile, and callous. Every moment you make a habit of practicing acceptance, you get to acknowledge how you feel while also choosing to leave the bitter emotions associated with it behind.

Acceptance doesn't justify every experience as being *right,* nor does it lessen the impact something has had on your life; it just holds space for your truth. No more pretending you are okay, no more denying your experience, and no more ignoring your feelings. All truth.

ACCEPTANCE AND RECLAIMING YOUR PEACE

One of the goals of acceptance is to be able to move forward with your life. But it's hard to do that when you can't seem to make peace with what happened in your past. Peace can feel like an abstract at times—we can't just jump into it. But when you practice small habits of acceptance—seeing people for who they are, adjusting your expectations, and actively leaving the past behind— you will slowly reclaim the calming assurance of peace.

Acceptance is another habit that is important to view as a process: Wounds run deep, and true healing takes time. Sometimes it's not your past that keeps hurting you; it's the things you're struggling to accept in your day-to-day. By making daily choices that protect and add to your peace, you're practicing a nourishing habit that will sustain your healing.

FIVE STEPS TO BEGIN PRACTICING ACCEPTANCE DAILY

1. **Cross expired goals off your list.** Goal setting is a valuable practice, but when you keep goals that are no longer aligned with who you are or goals you don't have the capacity to fulfill, you ignore opportunities to succeed at other things.

2. **Reject comparison.** Seeing someone else's relationship, career, body, financial status, or background as better than yours robs you of your own unique journey. Accept that you can't have anyone else's life, and work to create your version of success.

   Take a moment to write down your unique characteristics. I always have clients write down their unique traits that they don't see in anyone else they know. One client wrote, "I don't mind cleaning up a mess. I like my space clean—even if it means I'm the one who has to keep it that way. I'm the queen of clean!" What are you the queen of?

3. **Stop questioning where you are in life.** There is no such thing as "You are *supposed* to be [fill in the blank] by now." Right now, you might not have everything you need to be prepared for where you're going next. Don't rush the process. Accept where you are and lean into your own pace. You will get married, have children, earn a degree, and work at your dream job in due time. Trust the timing of your life. Take advantage of this season of preparation.

Think about it. What can you improve? Finish this sentence: *I can use this time to improve my . . .*

What do you still need to learn? Finish this sentence: *I still need to learn to . . .*

Which one of your relationships needs your attention? Finish this sentence: *Now is a good time to work on my relationship with . . .*

4. **Honor your weaknesses.** This may be a surprising habit, but accepting where you fall short opens you up to opportunities to build community, expand your knowledge, and focus on your strengths. Ask for help, work on your personal development, and increase your proficiency in things you are already good at instead of pretending you are okay or trying to DIY your way through life.

My favorite way to practice this habit is to spend an entire day asking for help, even for the little things. Sometimes I ask for help choosing which coffee to order, fixing a minor technical issue while working in Microsoft Word, or opening a jar of spaghetti sauce for dinner. When I do this, I experience a day full of more ease. I can't do it all, and I am grateful I don't have to.

5. **Celebrate the small things you do well every day.** Celebrate getting to work on time, packing your own lunch, remembering to return a phone call or text, or not throwing an adult tantrum during afternoon traffic.

When things aren't going as planned, and it feels hard to celebrate, try creating a list of all the things you will do when you overcome the imperfection. This takes the focus off the failed plans, relationships, or circumstances and directs it toward a desired outcome.

THINGS YOU DON'T HAVE TO ACCEPT

We've discussed many things you may want to accept, but I can't close this chapter without addressing a few things it may *not* serve you to accept.

It may not serve you to accept mistreatment from your parents, even if you choose to accept who they are as people.

It may not serve you to accept a relationship with an abusive or disengaged partner.

It may not serve you to accept mistreatment or unfair conditions at work just because others say it "comes with the job."

Acceptance should not

- Require you to betray yourself

- Take away from your well-being

- Cause emotional or physical harm

- Be a response to manipulation or coercion

- Be something you do out of fear

A MOMENT OF SACRED PAUSE

In this chapter we've redefined acceptance, examined what it would look like to practice acceptance of things from the past (as far back as childhood), and learned how to practice acceptance in the day-to-day. Now it's time to fully embrace the practice.

For those who are reflecting on circumstances your younger self endured, be gentle and remember to breathe as you go back in time, while also remaining present as the version of yourself that you are now. Let your breath ground you. Remember you have already survived, remember you are fully in control, and remember to go only as deep as you can handle, at a pace that you determine.

For the exercises that follow, you can write your answers in a journal or you can audio journal your answers by using a recording application on your phone. Creating a written or audio record will capture the moment you're in so you can pace yourself, taking breaks as needed.

PROMPTS FOR ACCEPTANCE

What do you need to accept? Are there experiences from your childhood that you need to witness for what they were? Are you ruminating over what could've or should've been? Is there a parent or friend that you need to accept for who they are? Do you need to accept some things about your partner (or not accept them and move on)?

Why do you need to accept those things? Will you find peace? Will it improve your relationship with a parent? Will it give you closure about how you were raised as a child, about how a relationship with an ex had to end, or about a dream or goal that continues to go unfulfilled? And will it help you move forward?

What does acceptance look like? Will you release certain expectations of people? Will you end a relationship? Can acceptance lead
to the pursuit of a new and better experience in life, love, or your
career? Will your feelings of bitterness be replaced with peace?

*How will you practice the habit of acceptance today, this week, and/
or this month? What are the actions you can commit to doing?* Will you
schedule an appointment with a therapist? Can you make a small
promise to yourself? Do you need to block some people? Do you
need to reflect on why you're resisting acceptance?

USE THE SPACE BELOW TO WORK
THROUGH THE PROMPTS ON YOUR OWN

Need: _____

_____

_____

Why do I need to do this? _____

_____

_____

Healing Habits: _____

_____

_____

Practices/Action: _____

_____

_____

AFFIRMATIONS FOR ACCEPTANCE

Say this out loud with me:

I make peace with the story of my life.
I release bitterness and make room for better.
I am courageous enough to accept when something has
ended.
What didn't happen wasn't supposed to.
I trust the plan for my life.

Chapter 5

THE HABIT OF KNOWING YOUR LIMITS: HOW SELF-FORGIVENESS HEALS OUR RELATIONSHIP WITH PROGRESS

I sat down on the couch, exhausted and achy, and swung my legs around to elevate them. When I looked down, I noticed something unusual: My legs were extremely swollen. I brushed it off at first, because I had just finished cleaning the kitchen after cooking and hosting an entire Thanksgiving meal for close to fifty people. I figured I was just tired and so were my legs.

That morning, I had woken up before dawn to start cooking— just like my grandmom had always done. Turkey, ham, roast beef, collard greens, string beans, mashed potatoes, candied yams, baked macaroniandcheese (one word, according to soul-food tradition), turkey *and* beef gravy, and dressing (or stuffing, depending on where you're from) were cooked to perfection. This is still the proudest moment in my cooking career because no one believed I'd cooked all the food myself. Not only was the food so good that everyone thought my grandmom must have helped me; it was also hot and ready to eat by 2 P.M. sharp. This was a standard my grandmom had set and was the only one to maintain up to that point.

At the end of a sixteen-hour day, feeling exhausted and achy didn't surprise me—but the swelling did. By the time I saw the doctor about four days later, my ankles and feet had also swollen. I couldn't wear a closed shoe—just slides—and walking had become painful.

After months of testing, seeing specialists, and sending my medical records to a team at Columbia University, I was diagnosed with an autoimmune-based chronic kidney disease. At the moment of my diagnosis, I was devastated and terrified—but also relieved.

You see, months earlier, I had started to experience rapid weight gain. At that time, it made no sense. I was in the best shape of my life. Then, in a matter of weeks, I started to see my weight increase by five pounds, and then ten pounds, and then fifteen pounds. My doctor told me that I was probably overeating without realizing it, even though everyone in my life could attest to the fact that I wasn't eating much at all.

I was so mad at myself for gaining weight, and I was also discouraged by my lack of energy. I kept thinking it was my fault—that I was just being lazy. Ultimately, I felt relief to know that my weight gain and fatigue were caused by an identifiable medical issue, but I would go on to battle that issue for fourteen years. Now, instead of having to learn to forgive myself for gaining weight, I had to forgive myself for being down on myself during a time when I needed to be lifted the most.

DEFINING FORGIVENESS

Forgiveness has become a new F word in today's culture. Cutting people off or leaving people behind has grown to be the norm when someone has wronged you, and the idea of forgiving those "who trespass against us" can be labeled as *toxic*. The good news is that our culture is leaning into collective and individual healing, and with that comes a new appreciation for holding people accountable and enforcing consequences. We are taking our time with our hearts and carefully deciding if fighting for reconciliation, as well as forgiveness, is the best option or if we are risking further emotional damage.

But some people can take assigning consequences too far. As forgiveness is becoming increasingly taboo, we've been neglecting grace. The truth is that most of us are doing the best we can. We respond to what's going on in our lives based on past experiences and the options we have in front of us. When we find ourselves not making the best choices and engaging in unhealthy behaviors or connections, there is usually a source for our actions. Instead of only applying pressure to make immediate change, we might need to apply some grace and forgiveness. But forgiveness can be difficult to demonstrate, because so many of us have different definitions of what it is and different experiences of what a healthy expression of it looks like.

Alicia was taught to forgive without a second thought. And she did. She forgave as a spiritual practice, believing that doing so would keep her in good standing with God.

However, there was internal resistance that caused her emotional dissonance. This began years ago when Alicia forgave her father for cheating on her mother, leaving her as a witness in the back seat of the car as he dropped off gifts to his mistress. Alicia was young but carried that memory with her into adulthood—along with anxiety around being in committed relationships and receiving gifts. Years later, when her mother found out about the cheating, her mother forgave her father. Alicia revisited the moment she forgave her father in the past and realized that she forgave in practice, but in her heart there was still no trust.

Tanisha learned the hard way that there are consequences when we forgive people too easily. She told me a story about her childhood friend who once shared a secret about her life. That secret made its way around the whole school, and Tanisha was mortified. Her friend came to her crying and begged for forgiveness. So Tanisha forgave her—only to be betrayed again by that friend years later. The lesson Tanisha internalized was that if someone hurts you once, they'll hurt you again. In her experience, people didn't deserve forgiveness. Tanisha's idea was to protect herself with a one-and-done mindset. By the time she started coming to our sessions, Tanisha told me that she didn't have anyone in her life that she would call a friend—she had already cut everyone off.

Tatty didn't have a set rule around forgiveness. She told me that she judged each situation according to its own merit. If forgiveness was appropriate, she forgave. If she didn't think someone was truly sorry or had learned their lesson, she believed they deserved a consequence, so she severed the relationship. Tatty felt her practices were just—until people started to subvert her expectations. Her sibling, whom she had recently forgiven, had just hurt her again, and her ex—to whom she hadn't shown forgiveness—had just shown up for her and her family in the most generous way after her father's death. Tatty was confused about the role of forgiveness in her life.

OUR RESISTANCE TO SELF-FORGIVENESS

For years, even while working as a social worker, my conversations around the subject of forgiveness were pointed in the direction of *them*. Should we forgive *them*? Can you forgive *them*? This is how you forgive *them*.

Alicia, Tanisha, and Tatty took different approaches to forgiving others, just as many of the stories we hear about forgiveness are about forgiving other people. So it's helpful to start by defining what forgiveness means. In my work, I've found that it's increasingly difficult to find examples of *self*-forgiveness unless you're in a therapy session or attending a wellness seminar. Because the narrative of self-forgiveness is a fairly new addition to the conversation, it's common for people to internalize every bad thing that happens as something they need to forgive someone *else* for. Either way, when people choose to see forgiveness as an *F* word, they withhold forgiveness from everyone—including themselves.

Mr. Smith, as I'll call him, was a particularly interesting client. He was an inmate in his late twenties serving time for drug and gun convictions. Mr. Smith was near the end of his sentence when I met him.

For three or four months, Mr. Smith met with me for weekly counseling sessions, attended monthly group meetings, and participated in classes I led that were designed to decrease recidivism. He spent most of his sessions trying to convince me that he wasn't to blame for the actions that led to his incarceration—everyone else was. His father worked all the time. His brother thought he was better than him. His child's mother was left jaded by the men who came before him.

But in his mind, Mr. Smith's mother was the biggest offender of them all. She was cold, liked his brother more than him, spent all his father's money on herself and his brother, and never liked Mr. Smith or wanted him for a son.

Mr. Smith felt that his mother drove him to act out. He acted out only because she withheld her attention from him otherwise. He sold drugs only because she wouldn't give him any money. He wanted a lot of money to prove he could acquire more in life than his brother. And because his actions led to a criminal record that prevented him from getting the kind of job he wanted, he continued to do what he *had* to do to take care of his daughter. Mr. Smith's mindset was clear: He was the ultimate victim.

Every session started with him expressing anger about his mother and ended with him struggling with his daughter's anger against him. Mr. Smith thought his daughter's mother must have poisoned her against him, because she was a daddy's girl before he "went away." Now that he was in prison, he felt emotional distance between them. She was acting out and throwing blame in his direction. Mr. Smith couldn't handle that.

For weeks, he never asked my opinion or wanted any insight. He just vented the same story repeatedly. Part of my job was to listen, so that's what I did. Until, one day, he asked, "You're a woman, Mrs. Homer. What do you think?"

I had been waiting for the invitation. So, I leaned forward and asked the question that had been on my mind for months: "Are you scared your daughter will eventually feel about you the way you feel about your mother?"

It was all so evident to me. Mr. Smith held his mother to a standard that he'd failed to uphold himself, and deep down, he couldn't deal with that disconnect. He wanted to be forgiven, but receiving forgiveness would require him to see his own need to forgive.

He sat with that question for three minutes and sixteen seconds. (I know because I counted using the timer I set for our session.) Finally, his eyes started to well up, and a single tear fell from his left eye.

I don't think that tear was for himself. He was crying for his mother and his daughter. He began to shake his head before catching the tear with his hand. That was a breakthrough for Mr. Smith. I cried for him, too.

After a few weeks of sessions like this, Mr. Smith began to realize that he was being just as hard on his mother as he was afraid his daughter would be on him. He came to see how he was projecting his insecurities, shortcomings, and assumptions onto others, while simultaneously trying to dodge those things being projected back at him. And over time, Mr. Smith admitted that he lacked the awareness and maturity needed to communicate with those he loved. He had been filling that deficit the best way he knew how—with anger.

Like Mr. Smith, you may find yourself failing to meet the standards you set for yourself and others. Maybe you are a parent now and you realize

> *You may want to forgive yourself for*
>
> - *Breaking promises to yourself*
> - *Your contribution to a negative relationship*
> - *Putting yourself in compromising positions*
> - *Not achieving certain goals*
> - *Perceived weaknesses*

how your parents might have fallen short of their obligations at times because of difficulties they had to work through, like poverty, addiction, or mental health. Because of how you were raised, you may have set standards for yourself to live a certain lifestyle or acquire certain things that are ideal in best-case scenarios, but your circumstances and lack of access to resources and support make those standards unrealistic. It is especially during those times of falling short that you need to apply grace and extend forgiveness to yourself.

WHY SELF-FORGIVENESS MATTERS

Although difficult to practice, forgiving others is pretty straightforward. Either you forgive or you don't—and if you choose not to forgive, you can choose not to have a relationship with that person at all.

Self-forgiveness, though, is more complicated. You can choose

not to practice it, but the relationship with yourself is eternal—
and so are the consequences of choosing not to forgive yourself.

If you abstain from self-forgiveness, you may begin to store negative feelings toward yourself in your heart. Those feelings have
the potential to become self-sabotaging behaviors, especially if
deep down you believe that making mistakes means you don't
deserve to have good things happen for you. Denying yourself forgiveness means you deny yourself the benefit of a fresh start. The
self-denial might manifest as internalizing negative self-talk or
even talking badly about yourself in front of others. It could also
present as withholding moments of pleasure or basic self-care
from yourself because you don't believe you deserve it. And if this
behavior continues, you run the risk of bitterness, self-contempt,
and resentment taking root in you.

There is a fine line between self-correction and self-criticism.
Of course, it's helpful to acknowledge our mistakes and choose to
correct them. It is necessary to be aware of shortcomings or weak-
nesses. But sometimes that self-awareness can turn into destructive criticism, which leads to vigilance, which leads to perfectionism, which can lead to self-loathing. We might intend to be our best selves, but we slowly adopt a standard of perfection that sets the bar at an unrealistic height. It's one thing to want to be good at what you do, but it becomes problematic when you label
yourself as inherently bad the moment you fall short of your own
standard. Having a healthy habit of self-forgiveness will keep bit-

> *You will know you've crossed the line when you*
>
> - *Can't get past a mistake you've made*
> - *Engage in consistent negative self-talk*
> - *Bash yourself in front of others*
> - *Punish yourself by withholding good things from yourself*
> - *Project how you feel about yourself onto others*

terness, self-contempt, and resentment from becoming behaviors and mindsets that stunt your own progress.

WHAT SELF-FORGIVENESS HEALS IN US

Your capacity is your ability to perform, hold, contain, absorb, withstand, produce, understand, and do something. Your expectations of yourself must always meet your capacity. Capacity is limited, inconsistent, and subject to change.

I want you to think of capacity simply as ability. Were you *able* to maintain a healthy relationship with your partner? Were you *able* to show up for your friends the way you'd like? Were you *able* to complete the degree program you started? Were you *able* to hold down the position at work?

Most of the things we struggle to forgive within ourselves are shortcomings that happened when we didn't have the ability to fulfill them. Before you criticize yourself, pause and ask, "Did I have the capacity to get this right?" When the answer is "No," lean into the habit of self-forgiveness.

To be clear, acknowledging your capacity and forgiving your shortcomings is not an excuse to live a mediocre life. There are consequences to not performing well, and there is nothing wrong with maintaining standards for yourself. The goal is to have the standard *meet* your capacity—and you can increase your capacity at any time. This reframe helped me forgive myself for allowing my heart to be broken by the same person, twice.

When I was young, I wasn't practicing any of the habits for healing I write about in this book. I wasn't practicing self-care, I wasn't being accountable to myself for my actions, I wasn't accepting the truth about the status of my relationship, and I was refusing to fully let go. All the signs were there. My partner and I had emotional distance and inconsistencies, and my intuition was louder than ever. I knew we were growing apart, but the relation-ship was familiar, and I felt safe when things were good. I couldn't bring myself to put an end to this cycle of on-again, off-again, so my ex broke it for me instead (and with it, my heart one last time). When that happened, I was more upset with *myself* than I was with the ending of the relationship. I couldn't help but think of myself as stupid, a sucker, and desperate. For a few years, I wouldn't even let my heart consider a new love. To be honest, I didn't even trust myself with my own heart, so there was no way I was going to trust it with anyone else.

Forgiving myself began with examining my own capacity. At the time of this heartbreak, I was operating as if I were at full capacity. In actuality, I was depleted. I was using all my energy to show up as a full-time student who was also working a full-time job and dealing with family members battling addictions, mental health issues, and court cases. I had migraines daily. I had no social life. My relationship, although it wasn't perfect, was my only healthy escape at the time. I was doing the best I could. Later, I would learn how a few small adjustments to my mindset could com-pletely transform my relationship with my capacity.

DAILY WAYS TO PAY ATTENTION TO YOUR CAPACITY

- **Notice your sleep habits.** Are you getting enough rest to perform your duties to work, parent, or connect with your friends and partner well? Inadequate sleep inter-feres with your ability to think critically, decreases stam-ina, and decreases motivation.

- **Notice your mental and emotional state.** Do you feel anxious, stressed, or sad? Pay attention to the root of those feelings, and how they feel in your body. Emotional labor can impact your capacity by causing you to be moody, short-tempered, and distant with others.

- **Notice your eating habits.** Could your cravings, sudden changes in tolerance for certain foods, or nutritional deficits be signs of an internal issue that is disrupting the connection between your mind and your body? Have you noticed changes in your weight, skin appearance, and body shape? Sometimes it's not just a bad habit of snacking. Sometimes the root of your dysregulation could be your mental health or another health condition.

- **Notice your environment.** Are you spending lots of time around people, places, and things that have a negative influence on your thoughts and actions? Who have you been in communication with? What are you watching on television or social media? How are things in your community? Keep in mind that your input directly affects your output.

- **Notice your self-talk.** What you say to yourself is an indication of how you feel about yourself, your life, and your choices. Sometimes you don't hate yourself; you just hate where you are in life. Maybe you hate your job, where you live, your relationship, or your financial status. Be careful to avoid misdirecting these negative emotions toward someone that doesn't deserve it—*you.*

Ultimately, checking in on your capacity is an act of self-compassion. Instead of judging yourself harshly for how you think, perform, and make decisions, you can look behind the scenes and identify what is negatively impacting your ability to show up for yourself. Once you begin to forgive yourself and make adjustments that increase your capacity, you'll be a better advocate for yourself.

SELF-FORGIVENESS AND RECLAIMING YOUR PEACE

What I love about the habit of self-forgiveness is that it helps us eject from counterintuitive cycles. When you become aware of the presence of self-loathing, you can actively work toward forgiveness, evolve to be a better version of yourself, and practically reclaim your peace.

> *You engage in an act of self-forgiveness every time you*
>
> * *Maintain your health through regular checkups*
> * *Align your environment to meet your physical, emotional, and spiritual needs*
> * *Use words of affirmation to combat negative self-talk*
> * *Say yes only to things you are good at doing (or work to get better at something you want to do)*
> * *Try again after a failure once you've gained the education and insight needed to succeed*

There will be times when your intentions are well-meaning, but the impact will not reflect that. It is impossible to make it through life without doing something you regret. Coming down on yourself every time you fall short only strengthens the feelings of guilt and shame. It reinforces the belief that you are a bad person, and therefore unworthy of the life you desire.

Hear me when I say that you are worth more than every mistake you've ever made. Your past is relevant only when it helps you or someone else. Once you begin to practice the habit of self-forgiveness, you'll be able to truly believe that.

* Through self-forgiveness, you get to make mistakes without allowing them to define who you are as a person.

- Through self-forgiveness, you are not disqualified after the first failed attempt; you get more chances to get things right.

- Through self-forgiveness, your feeling of wholeness can be restored as you leave guilt and shame behind.

Self-forgiveness brings peace to the internal war you have with yourself every time you make a mistake. Let self-forgiveness demonstrate how mistakes can be an incredible reminder of your humanity, and the habit of forgiveness can be an opportunity to show yourself empathy and compassion—which are crucial ingredients to reclaiming a foundation of peace in your life.

FIVE MORE STEPS TO BEGIN THE HABIT OF SELF-FORGIVENESS

1. **Acknowledge what you did.** I had a client named Ashlee who blew through her entire savings because she was trying to keep up with the lifestyle of her new friends. Afterward, when she was trying to backpedal from her financial losses, she punished herself by refusing to buy *anything* she wanted—not even a bridesmaid dress for her sister's wedding. When she took a step back and examined her emotional capacity, she realized that deep inside she was acting out of a desperate desire for belonging, having never felt like she fit into the family she was adopted into at eight years old. All along, she was trying to buy love, which wasn't a mere act of reckless spending. Those actions during that time in her life had deep layers that she

needed to acknowledge before she could work hard to heal and forgive herself.

Acknowledging what your level of capacity was when you did what you did helps you move through it with less judgment, shame, and self-disdain, and ultimately provides you with an objective view of your role in the situation.

2. **Acknowledge your feelings.** Mr. Smith, from earlier in this chapter, is an example of what life can look like when you deny your true feelings. He was hurt by how he felt his mother treated him. Whether her actions were intentionally harmful or not, the impact on Mr. Smith was very real. He didn't have the mental or emotional capacity to deal with it on his own, but through our work together he was able to uncover feelings of abandonment, fear, judgment, and inadequacy. By acknowledging these feelings, he was able to move forward and forgive his mother and himself, and eventually seek the forgiveness of his daughter and her mother.

3. **Make amends/apologize to yourself.** An apology to yourself can be a beautiful act of compassion and empathy for the impact your own actions have had on your life. It's a powerful act of accountability and can be soothing to your central nervous system. If you write down the apology and then read it, especially out loud in your own voice, doing so sends a message that you are no longer interested in being at war with yourself over what you've done in the past. I write "Dear Self" letters often, not just when I am extending an apology, but also when I want to express gratitude for the other ways I show up for myself.

4. **Self-correct/make changes.** Practicing daily acts of forgiveness using the list I shared earlier (page 90) is a great place to start changing your behavior. Doing things like noticing and adjusting your capacity, trying again after a failure, and combating negative self-talk with daily affirmations is how you *show* yourself that you are sorry. When I would tell my grandmom I was sorry for doing something I shouldn't have done, like staying up too late or talking back (as she would call it), she'd say, "Act like it." That was her way of saying an apology should be accompanied by changed behavior. These days, I say the same thing to my son when he apologizes, and now I am saying the same to you. When you are sorry, *act like it.*

5. **Apply grace/practice compassion as many times as you need to.** Please understand that self-forgiveness is a lifelong practice, and you will no doubt fall short again and again. With every attempt at becoming the person you are meant to be comes the risk of not getting it right. Remember that you are a human being who responds to life the best way you know how. Instead of seeing self-forgiveness as the thing you have to do because you failed, see it as something you get to practice because you tried.

WHAT THE HEALING HABIT OF SELF-FORGIVENESS CAN LOOK LIKE

After working with Me'Chele for twelve weeks, I realized that she was still struggling to forgive herself for the years she spent addicted to drugs and alcohol—a condition that ruined her marriage and ended her first career. She had been in recovery for ten years, started a new, successful career in New York City, and turned her entire life around. Now she was sponsoring other addicts, mentoring her niece, and supporting her elderly parents financially.

Despite countless stories she knew of people who were not as successful at changing, Me'Chele struggled to give herself the credit she deserved and forgive herself. So, I started opening our sessions by asking her, "How did you practice forgiveness this week?"

Me'Chele started small. "Well, I got over missing the train this morning because I was running late." "I forgot my lunch and had to eat out today, but I didn't mind." In one session, before I got a chance to ask my question, Me'Chele said, "Today marks ten years sober. I'm old!" as she laughed and took a sip of her coffee. I said, "Well, getting to say 'I'm old' is a blessing for someone with your history." Me'Chele began to cry. After she composed herself, she said, "I always thought I would die. I waited for the day, and it never happened. Wow . . ." Me'Chele cried a little more.

Self-forgiveness is a sacred act of healing. It is the ultimate expression of self-love and self-care for those who have had to survive and overcome a difficult past. When you find yourself leaning back into negative self-talk or operating outside of your capacity again (and judging yourself for it), come back to this chapter. Let it serve as a reminder that you are doing the best you can, and forgive yourself again and again.

PROMPTS FOR SELF-FORGIVENESS

What do you need to forgive yourself for? Explore your feelings of guilt and shame to uncover areas of your life where you need to apply some grace. Do you feel guilty for how you behaved in a relationship that ended poorly? Are you ashamed of the current state of your mental or physical health?

Why do you need to forgive those things? Have guilt and shame prevented you from going after the life you want? Has self-criticism deemed you unworthy? How can forgiving yourself improve the quality of your life?

What does forgiveness look like? Will you pardon yourself from a lifetime sentence of unworthiness and reclaim your regard for yourself? Can you pair this healing habit with self-care, acceptance, and letting go?

How will you practice the habit of self-forgiveness today, this week, and/or this month? What are the actions you can commit to doing? What can you do to work through the shame today? Can you issue an apology to someone you've offended? Will you write yourself a letter of apology?

USE THE SPACE BELOW TO WORK
THROUGH THE PROMPTS ON YOUR OWN

Need: _____

_____

_____

Why do I need to do this? _____

_____

_____

Healing Habits: _____

_____

_____

Practices/Action: _____

_____

_____

AFFIRMATIONS FOR SELF-FORGIVENESS

Say this out loud with me:

I am worthy of forgiveness.
I release my feelings of guilt and shame.
I give myself as many chances as I need to get it right.
I apply grace and forgiveness to the moments I fall short.
I am worth more than every mistake I've ever made.

Chapter 6

THE HABIT OF DAILY INVESTIGATION: HOW NOT TAKING THINGS PERSONALLY HEALS OUR RELATIONSHIP WITH TRUTH

For years, I woke up every morning between 3:50 and 4:15 to get to the gym by 5 A.M. This habit started out of necessity. I needed to work out because, *health . . .* and the only time I could do that was before the kids got up. Most days, I pulled into the parking lot before the employees even got there to open the door.

I am not a morning person. It's early, I'm up—but I'm not a chirping-bird kind of girl. I like mornings to be slow, dark, and silent. Not total silence (there is no way I could make it through a workout without music), but talking and socializing with others has never been something I could get into before the light of day.

If you've never been to the gym at 5 A.M., you should know that not many people are there. Most of them who are, are of a seasoned age (that's my way of saying old folk). Once the door opens, everyone usually walks in and does their own thing. But while we wait for the employees to open the door and everyone strolls to their stations, the seasoned folks are pretty social. They greet one another with smiles, hellos, and head nods. They chat about new gym shoes and colorful leggings. They cheer on progress and welcome newcomers. And after a few weeks of witnessing what life looks like for morning people who get to the gym at 5, I noticed something: No one was being social with me.

I promise you, I had no real desire to be talkative so early in the morning, but something about not having the option didn't sit well with me. For weeks after noticing that I was apparently being excluded, I started to pay close attention to who said hello to whom. I wondered if no one spoke to me because I'm young, or maybe they could hear the rap music blaring from my head-phones, or maybe it's because I'm Black. Yes, I took it *there*. When I finally mentioned my concerns to a friend, she reminded me that as a non–morning person, I most likely walked in looking like the last thing I wanted to be was sociable.

I put her theory to the test the very next day. I walked up to the gym entrance with no headphones on and a smile on my face, and immediately got a smile back from one of the regulars. As I strolled to the locker room, I smiled again and another regular said, "Good morning." On the way out, I nodded my head and the person walking in nodded back. I shook my head at myself, thinking about how offended I'd been, about the stories I had come up with, and about how personally I took not being included in the early morning camaraderie. Turns out, I was getting what I put out.

DEFINING TAKING THINGS PERSONALLY

We take things personally when we attribute an outcome, experience, or opinion from someone else directly to ourselves.

Sometimes we do this because we've considered only our own perspective on the situation. Other times, it's because we're projecting our worldview onto others and making assumptions about their motivations. Maybe someone didn't hold the door for you on the way out of the grocery store, and you label them as rude instead of considering the possibility that they didn't see you, were distracted by someone else walking in, or maybe couldn't extend their arm due to a recent injury. Maybe you labeled a sales associate as unenthusiastic because they weren't smiling, but maybe they were just processing bad news, like having their hours cut.

Sometimes we don't even need another person's involvement to take things personally. Maybe you forgot a friend's birthday, so you labeled yourself a horrible friend instead of viewing it as a mistake you made. In that scenario, you've framed your mistake as a testament to your character—who you are as a person—not merely an action that you've mistakenly done.

When you internalize every interaction with someone, every opinion shared, and every mistake made, it can affect every area of your life. You send messages to yourself and others that you are a victim. You give others the power to determine if you feel good or bad about yourself. And ultimately, other people and things will have more power over your life than you do.

> *Taking things personally can*
>
> * *Diminish your regard for yourself*
> * *Leave you vulnerable to offense*
> * *Give you a negative outlook on life*
> * *Cultivate a poor attitude*
> * *Create problems where there were none*

When we practice the habit of not taking things personally, we open the door to greater clarity, fewer grievances, and fewer opportunities to be offended. This habit gives us freedom from the pressure of thinking that everything is about us. It breaks the unhealthy cycle of changing who we are or compromising our values because we're obsessed with the need to be right, or validated, or accepted.

IT MAY HAVE NOTHING TO DO WITH YOU

Shelly was excited about being a grandmother. Her son and daughter-in-law had been married for five years when they shared the news that they were expecting their first child. Everyone on both sides of the family was eager to welcome the baby into their world.

Shelly was an it-takes-a-village-to-raise-a-child kind of grandmother. She assured her daughter-in-law, Brooke, that she would be supported in every way and took it upon herself to start planning and preparing for the baby's arrival. Shelly started ordering furniture and other gifts, planning future family gatherings, and doing many other things Brooke never asked her to do.

This activity went on until Brooke was about six months pregnant and decided she needed to address what felt like invasive and overbearing behavior. When Shelly attempted to take charge of planning Brooke's baby shower, Brooke politely declined the offer. Shelly was offended, and eventually she reached out to me for advice.

Immediately, it was clear to me that Shelly and Brooke had two different perspectives on the role a mother-in-law should play in their family. Based on the information I was given, it seems Brooke entertained Shelly's perspective until it felt like her own wasn't being considered. Brooke wasn't declining Shelly personally; she was declining her offer to take over an occasion that clearly meant something to her.

During our first conversation, I asked Shelly if Brooke already had plans for her baby shower. She didn't know. I asked Shelly if any of Brooke's family or friends—perhaps her own mother—wanted to participate in the planning. She didn't know. I asked Shelly if she consulted with her own son about his wishes for the baby shower or any other plans for the baby. She said no. Slowly, it dawned on Shelly that not only was she taking it personally that Brooke had declined her offer, but she had made the entire baby experience about her.

Take this from Shelly: Not everything you experience in life is about you. It's not bad to be invested in something, but there are other people, with other perspectives, desires, goals, and ideas, that you should consider before taking control of a situation. One of the beauties of being in relationships with others is that we get the benefit of other opinions, wisdom, and experiences. Considering others opens you up to their world, and not taking things personally allows people to be seen and heard.

> *These things are not personal and *they may still hurt*
>
> * *Being let go from a job*
> * *Being passed over for a promotion*
> * *Not being someone's dating preference*
> * *Someone breaking up with you*
> * *Someone's negative opinion about your performance, gifts, or talents*
> * *Someone declining your offer of any kind*

RESISTANCE TO NOT TAKING THINGS PERSONALLY

It's natural to care about what people think. You want to know if the people you love love you back. It's okay to care about how you are seen by friends and family. And nobody wants to be judged unfavorably by their boss, colleagues, or peers. So, when someone offends you, projects onto you, or declines your offers, you experience involuntary emotional responses. These feelings are unavoidable. We are wired as humans to feel, and sometimes the things we shouldn't take personally still hurt.

Certain life experiences can also leave you vulnerable to internalization and desperate to appease others. You may take things personally, hoping that you can sway the opinion or thoughts others have about you in your favor. If you've struggled with the following vulnerabilities, you may have a resistance to not taking things personally:

- **Childhood trauma.** Did you have a lack of emotional support when you were most impressionable? Were you blamed for the consequences others faced and forced to take responsibility for other people's happiness, or lack thereof? Did you grow up bullied by adults or peers? If any of these things are true, you may tend to create a narrative that you deserve to be treated poorly—and that everything others say about you is true. Children who were *parentified* (obligated to act as a parent to their own parents or siblings) often struggle with taking things personally.

- **Low regard/self-esteem.** If you regularly experience low self-esteem, you may find yourself dependent on validation from others. You may tend to view their opinions as facts, not suggestions. You may wait for permission to take action in your own life. You may change your mind about your relationships, career, and other lifestyle choices to fit the projection of people you want to please. Everything they say about you feels personal because it has a direct effect on your own regard for yourself.

- **Perfectionism.** If you are a perfectionist, you probably have unrealistic standards for yourself. This makes it hard to hear others talk about your flaws or even give constructive critiques without unconscious assimilation. For you, a critique is a cue to try harder to be perfect.

- **Feelings of overwhelm, stress, or fatigue.** When you are already at a deficit or not in the best mood, you may be more likely to misinterpret someone's comment, and think their opinion requires your response. Your emotional capacity might lead you to do whatever you need to do to quiet someone's opinion. You may find yourself going along to get along.

Whatever vulnerability you have struggled with, when your well-being is already compromised you will likely feel sensitive about what other people say or do to you. Although it's important to cultivate a habit of not taking things personally, don't feel bad about yourself when you give in to the opinions and projections of others. Instead, show grace to yourself first, and then learn to work through those feelings and separate what someone says about you from who you are.

FIGHTING THE RESISTANCE

It takes time to learn how to distinguish when something is personal and when it's not. To work on this habit, start with what I call the This or That Theory. If you're experiencing a particular situation where you might be feeling vulnerable to taking things personally, ask yourself, "Is it this or that?" That is, am I responding to what is happening in *this moment*—how I'm parenting, my job performance, or my relationship choice? Or am I reacting to *that time from the past*—when I lacked support, felt like a failure, and needed to prove myself? Do I have the proper perspective for *this* experience I am having right now, or am I caught up in *that* past moment that made me feel like who I am wasn't enough?

Take a moment to practice this exercise. If you uncover that you are reacting to the past, try making a conscious decision not to take it personally and respond more appropriately.

WHY NOT TAKING SOMETHING PERSONALLY MATTERS

What if how someone is treating you truly *is* personal? What if someone lies to you? What if someone betrays your trust? Undervalues you as an employee? Refuses to consider your perspective? Crosses your boundaries? Initially, I struggled with this habit because of those possibilities. Bear with me here: I believe that even when it truly *is* personal, it still may benefit you *not* to take the situation personally.

I've learned that most people do and say things based on their own needs, values, and internal deliberations. If you pay attention to how the offender treats other people in their lives, you might notice a pattern that reaches much further than how they interact with you. The situation is likely not entirely about you, but about how you can or cannot fulfill their current needs.

Not taking things personally matters because it teaches us about truth. This habit becomes a dance between standing in your own truth and leaving room for the truth of others. It teaches you how to feel things without judging yourself or the person who triggered the

> *Signs you are taking things too personally*
>
> - *You get defensive or angry easily.*
> - *You depend on the approval of other people to make you happy.*
> - *You see every mistake in behavior as a flaw in character.*
> - *You apologize without cause.*
> - *You obsess over interactions with others to the point where it interferes with your ability to move forward.*

feeling, and ultimately it helps you learn to separate who you are from what others say you are.

IT PENETRATES ONLY WHEN IT RESONATES

I make the most irresistible, delicious, soul-satisfying baked macaroniandcheese (remember, one word). Naturally, I learned it from my grandmom, the source of all my cooking skills. But over the years, what started out as her mac & cheese recipe evolved into a recipe of my own. Mine is creamier, richer, and somehow lighter despite the added spices and flavors. Don't get me wrong . . . I wouldn't dare say mine is better. I'm just saying it's good—and I'm not the only one to say it.

If someone were to try my mac & cheese and decide it wasn't good, I honestly wouldn't take it personally. This dish has already won the approval of my grandmom and countless other family members, friends, and colleagues. I have been paid to make pans of it to grace other people's holiday tables. If someone new came along and said it wasn't for them, I wouldn't internalize it one bit. I would serve my mac & cheese to Jesus himself without breaking a sweat. That's how confident I am in the dish.

You may read this and think yours is just as good, or maybe your grandmother's is better. But this is not about whose is better—it's about what I have already determined about my own.

The level of confidence I have in my dish cannot be penetrated. The same is true for everything you believe about yourself. This ranges from little things—like your ability to cook great food, write a best-selling book, make a winning shot in a basketball game, earn a perfect score on a test, or convince a potential client to work with your firm—to deeper things, like your belief in your right to a meaningful life despite your past mistakes, or to a healthy relationship despite your track record. Things penetrate through your beliefs and into your heart only if they already resonate some-where inside of you. It penetrates only when it resonates.

You can't get to me about my mac & cheese, but there are things that have been said about me that did get to me. Because of the insecurity I already felt about becoming a mom, I took it incredi-bly personally whenever someone commented on how I dressed my daughter. Even something like a simple remark from my grandmom about my daughter's coat not looking warm enough bothered me. In my head, I heard *Nakeia, you are a bad mom.* Growing up in poverty made me vulnerable to little jokes about my family's money or lifestyle. I internalized them to mean that *I* was a joke.

To undo those insecurities, I had to make a clear distinction between what I've experienced and who I am. Writing on small pieces of paper and sticky notes, I began listing attributes and personal characteristics that were true and evident about me. I listed qualities like being an overcomer and being resilient and persistent, and I kept those slips of paper in a jar so I wouldn't forget them. Then I journaled about my education and profes-sional accomplishments, and later I wrote about being a mother figure to my siblings, cousins, nieces, and nephews even at a young age. Eventually, the truth I wrote on that paper took root in my heart. Instead of internalizing outside opinions and projec-tions that I'd never measure up as a mother, I learned to embody the truth of who I was.

WHAT NOT TAKING THINGS PERSONALLY HEALS IN US

When you choose to see opinions from others as mere suggestions that are based on their own lives, you maintain a clear view of the truth of who you are. When you see someone's actions or behavior

toward you as an indication of their capacity—and not an indictment of their character or yours—you maintain a clear view of
what their truth is.

Not taking things personally keeps us connected to the truth.
Think about times in your past when you internalized a joke, the
end of a friendship, or getting turned down for a promotion. What
type of mental gymnastics did your mind perform? How did you
start to feel about yourself? Think about the assumptions you may
have made about a romantic partner not texting you back, or how
you felt the last time you didn't get invited to an event. How judgmental were you toward the people involved or even yourself?
How long were you obsessed with your own thoughts? Practicing
the habit of not taking things personally will prevent us from
wrecking our own peace with scenarios that may not even be true.

Instead of being consumed by assumptions, investigate every
situation to uncover the truth. Ask questions. Seek clarity. Stay
open to views outside of your own.

You will know you have landed on the truth when it aligns with
reality, not the stories in your head. Reality is rooted in facts and
backed by actual evidence. I heard this statement when I was in
my early twenties, and it stuck with me: *The truth will always stand
the test of investigation.*

It is healing to know the truth, even when the truth is painful.
The trick is, you get to that truth by asking directly.

*I am checking in on my application for employment. Are you still
considering me for the job?*

*When you didn't answer my text earlier, I became concerned that
you were avoiding me. Is everything okay between us?*

Direct questions tend to get direct answers. When you skip the
investigation and jump straight to conclusions, you reject yourself
before anyone has a chance to reject you. You may not be able to
investigate why someone cut you off in traffic, or why someone

didn't return a "hello" in the subway, but you can investigate your own projections, trace the source of those thoughts, and start healing them.

When I get cut off in traffic or someone doesn't greet me back, I get angry because I feel disrespected and invisible. I can't seem to shake this burning desire for recognition.

That reflection is an example of how our projections can be rooted in experiences that are possible to heal, if we take the time to trace them to the source. Although your feelings in the immediate moment are valid, they are not facts. Take this example a step further and consider your own experience with driving. No matter how amazing your car is, you don't always have a clear view of other drivers on the road. Don't assume you are invisible to someone who might not have seen you in the first place.

When we break down the facts in each specific situation, reality starts to defuse our inflated reactions. By taking a moment to reflect and then not take something personally, you're empowered to move on in peace with the rest of your day.

HOW THE HABIT OF NOT TAKING THINGS PERSONALLY HELPS US RECLAIM OUR PEACE

As a child, I lacked the emotional and intellectual capacity to understand the circumstances that led to my living with my grandmom and not my mom. I felt rejected, unwanted, unworthy, and not good enough. Even after growing older, getting all the details, and making peace with the fact that I had teenage parents who made the best decision they could for me at the time—the narrative I had in my head that I wasn't part of the plan and that I was a burden continued to trigger me.

I often joke about how unbelievable it is that almost every one of my professional endeavors had rejection built into it. From being a makeup artist, to a songwriter, to a well-being consultant, to an author, I've heard "no," "maybe next time," "we went with someone else," and even no response at all more times than I ever thought I could handle. To be honest, even writing this book was triggering. Having to revisit the moments in my life that inspired a need to heal reminded me of some of the narratives I've out-grown. Those old stories are still there, and I still hear them when-ever I'm hurt or disappointed. But now, I've learned to reclaim my peace from them.

Not taking things personally helps us reclaim our peace by blocking or regulating the negative emotions that spring up from internalized messages. When you understand the bias of perspec-tive and the role it plays in our actions and behaviors, you are mindful to investigate every situation to uncover the facts and get to the truth. With this habit, you finally allow others to feel what-ever it is they feel about you without taking on those feelings your-self. You learn to see things like rejection as part of the process of putting yourself out there and going after what you want in life, personally and professionally. And you stop allowing a single in-teraction with someone to define your whole life.

You will never be able to control what other people do or say, or whether they receive you into their lives as who you are. But you can choose to reject the habit of assumption, lean into the truth, and make peace with whatever that truth may be. You can choose what to internalize and what to disregard. You can treat each indi-vidual interaction with someone as a separate experience and not proof that you are wrong, bad, unworthy, or deserving of mistreat-ment. You can relieve yourself of the habits of defending yourself, trying to be right all the time, and working overtime to persuade others of your worth. You can choose peace instead.

We encounter people who have opinions every day on the job,

in our families and friend groups, and even on social media. Every day, there is an opportunity for you to reclaim your peace through the habit of not taking things personally.

FIVE STEPS TO BEGIN
NOT TAKING THINGS PERSONALLY

1. **Be curious.** Before internalizing an opinion or negative action from someone else, ask, "What else could it be?" This is also known as perspective-taking. Is there something outside of your own worldview that you could acknowledge?

   Try entertaining another perspective unless/until it is proven to be wrong. You may find that you were offended without cause.

   It's important to note here that sometimes your vibes are correct. Sometimes people are rude, dismissive, judgmental, and maybe just don't like you or your choices. Even then, my reminder to clients is *Don't take it personally. Take notes.* Be curious about their actions toward you, and be mindful to protect your peace when deciding how to respond.

   You may need to address the way someone is treating you, or you may choose to ignore them and live your life. Either way, you don't have to see their remarks as an indictment of you as a person. And you can choose not to respond to other people's insecurities. Are they judging you based on the parenting mistakes *they've* made? Are they picking on you to distract themselves and the rest of the family from the drama in their own life? Either way, it's not personal.

2. **Work through what already resonates.** We tend to take things we believe about ourselves to heart because they already live inside us in some form. You will know this is an issue when a comment from your boss about work reads as "I suck at this job" instead of "I should have proofed that document before turning it in." You make it about *you* and not the work. When your spouse doesn't eat their full plate of dinner because they had a big lunch, you may read this as "they don't appreciate me" if you are already unsatisfied with how you relate and communicate as a couple. Because of unmet needs and lack of self-awareness, you see offense in every interaction. Work through your feelings of unworthiness so you don't agree with others who try to deem you unworthy.

That work may look like

- Pausing to put some time between how you feel about what was said and how you respond

- Asking for clarity about the other person's comment or action

- Examining the feeling and naming it so you respond correctly

- Going through the prompts from the previous chapters and creating a list of positive attributes you can reference

3. **Consider the source.** Before doing the heavy lifting of processing your emotions and working through your feelings, consider this: Is the source of critique coming from someone you enjoy and respect? Does this person like you, or even know you well enough to have an opinion of

you? Does this person always have something negative to say about everything and everyone? A critique from someone you can trust will be constructive and mindful, not abrasive and inconsiderate of your feelings.

4. **Challenge your self-talk.** Taking things personally leaves us thinking untrue things like "I'm so stupid," "it's all my fault," or "they never appreciate me." The next time you find yourself ruminating like this, interrupt your automatic response by inserting positive words of affirmation into the process. Make a conscious effort to affirm: *I am not stupid for making a mistake, I am not responsible for someone else's thoughts or actions,* and *I am not my negative thoughts.* Challenge and replace your reflexive negative self-talk with positive affirmations.

5. **Adopt a spirit of excellence in everything you do.** This is something my early mentors introduced to me. Coming from what many consider a broken home, living in poverty, and often being the only Black person in my class or on the job, I felt like I had something to prove—probably because often, I did. So I began to work harder, study longer, and push further to fill in the gaps and disadvantages with skill, intellect, and talent. If anyone said I wasn't excellent in all my efforts, I'd know they were projecting lies. I knew the truth was evident.

If you show up as your best self and strive to be good in all that you do, you won't fall to the opinions of others because you'll be confident that you've given your all. Confidence isn't a by-product of perfection; it's a side effect of being excellent. Mastering a skill, developing a talent, studying an interest, and just uncovering ways to be a better you make it hard for something someone else says about you to penetrate.

When you get to decide what's worth spending your energy on, you maintain control of your projections and reactions, and you invite regular healthy interactions into your life.

Through curiosity, self-reflection, and habits that help you live your own truth, you create more peace in your life. You get to participate in your own healing.

PROMPTS FOR NOT TAKING THINGS PERSONALLY

What are some things you need to not *take personally?* Are there triggering opinions or unpleasant interactions in your relationships, on the job, or internally that you have been feeling hypersensitive about? What have you been saying about yourself lately? Is your self-talk typically negative? Spend some time practicing curiosity around your worldview and take note of where you need a change in perspective.

Why do you need to stop taking things personally? Will this help improve your performance at work or interaction with a co-worker because you have more clarity after being curious or showing empathy? Will this help decrease arguments in your relationships because you've addressed your insecurities and started embodying your strengths? Will not taking things personally decrease your worry over what people think of you?

What does not taking things personally look like? Will you start by acknowledging that there are alternatives to your perspective? Will you pause before internalizing things? Will you be less judgmental of yourself and others?

How will you practice the habit of not taking things personally today, this week, and/or this month? What are the actions you can commit to doing? Can you journal your emotional responses to critiques and decide what to take to heart and what to disregard? Can you create positive affirmations that challenge your negative self-talk? Can you explore your triggers and work to heal them through prayer, meditation, and therapy?

USE THE SPACE BELOW TO WORK
THROUGH THE PROMPTS ON YOUR OWN

Need: _____

_____

_____

Why do I need to do this? _____

_____

_____

Healing Habits: _____

_____

_____

Practices/Action: _____

_____

_____

AFFIRMATIONS FOR NOT TAKING THINGS PERSONALLY

Say this out loud with me:

Someone else's opinion is not my standard.
I release every harsh judgment I have of myself.
What someone else thinks of me lives inside their head, not
   mine.
I do not rise or fall because someone else says so.
I am curious about what others think, but not controlled
   by it.

PART THREE

RECLAIM YOUR POWER

The place in which I'll fit will not exist
until I make it.
—James Baldwin

Chapter 7

THE HABIT OF PROTECTING YOUR ENERGY: HOW MINDING YOUR BUSINESS HEALS YOUR RELATIONSHIP WITH FOCUS

Saturday afternoon shopping trips have always been a ritual for me and my daughter. From the early days of pushing her around department stores in her stroller as she grabbed ahold of pieces she liked and exclaimed, "Look, Mom! That's 'fashiony,'" to our more recent routine of walking shoulder to shoulder, window shopping while sipping on Starbucks—mall trips have always been a special time for us to connect.

One Saturday afternoon trip sticks out in my memory, and not just for the bonding. We had just moved to Atlanta, far away from my friends and family. Social media was a great way for me to stay connected—not to mention, get opinions from friends and followers on which outfit to buy. When we made the move to Georgia, I noticed that someone I knew from home also lived in the area, so I often scrolled through her posts and pictures, looking for things to do as I settled into southern living.

My daughter and I were heading to the food court to grab one of those must-have pretzels, and guess who I saw? Yes! It was the person from back home. She was with her daughter as well. We were hugging and doing the whole "OMG, it's been years" thing as we introduced our daughters. As I lowered my gaze to her little girl, I exclaimed, "Wow! She looks just like her father." A completely normal observation—except that I didn't know her father in real life. I'd only seen him in those pictures I scrolled through from time to time. The look on her face said, "How do *you* know what my husband looks like?"

My face got hot as I tried to explain, telling her about my scrolls through her account, and how I always notice when daughters look like their daddies because mine looks like hers. But the more I talked, the more I sounded like a stalker. She was looking at me sideways, and so was my daughter. I awkwardly excused myself from the little circle we had formed in front of Auntie Anne's and walked away. From that moment on, I decided to mind my own business.

WHAT IT MEANS TO MIND YOUR OWN BUSINESS

The phrase itself sounds harsh, but as a healing habit, "mind your business" is a gentle reminder to redirect your focus to yourself. Life is distracting enough. You have work to do. You have a purpose to fulfill. You have a past (or present) to heal. There are so many commitments that seem to pull us in every direction. Part of your healing work is to focus on the people and efforts that bring you more peace and joy and enable you to stay in your power. Nothing will do that for you better than avoiding the temptation to mind other people's business.

Minding other people's business looks like

- Making absolute statements about things that have absolutely nothing to do with you

- Getting so hyperfocused on what someone else has going on in their life that you neglect your own

- Prioritizing the peace, happiness, well-being, and successful outcomes of other people over your own

- Being more invested in the relationship, career, or health of another person than they are themselves

- Attempting to keep up with the lifestyle, relationship status, or career of others you admire

You can mean well and want what's best for others *and still* take things too far. Being consumed or preoccupied with someone else's life is where the line between supporting others and projecting is drawn.

RESISTANCE TO MINDING YOUR OWN BUSINESS

Social media has reprogrammed our ideas of what real life looks like. In real life, you ask your real friends which outfit to buy. In real life, only your close friends and family know who your spouse or partner is, and whether your child looks like them. But since many of us now live a portion of our lives online, real life has been expanded to include friends and followers from social media.

I have nothing against social media. Many of you are likely reading this book because that's where you discovered me and my work. Connecting with people online is valuable. You can find love, friendship, and career opportunities that evolve into real-life connections, or just remain connected on the internet and still feel a sense of belonging. But the rules can get fuzzy, and boundaries can be crossed.

Consider your specific relationship with social media:

- Have the websites or applications you use to consume content changed the way you view real life?

- Has the ability to peek into the lives of strangers influenced whom you consider a friend?

- Has receiving an invitation via social media to get all up in other people's business created an opportunity for you to connect with people in your head?

- Do you feel like you know those people enough to share your opinion or give unsolicited advice?

- Have your beliefs about your relationships, career, or yourself in general changed because of how you've been comparing them to your social media "friends"?

Social media is not entirely to blame for our inability to mind our own business. I come from the era when mamas and aunties would sit on the front porch gossiping and exchanging unsolicited advice while kids like me sat nearby pretending not to listen in. What was said on that porch stayed on that porch—whether it was an opinion on who shouldn't be dating whom, who was running low on funds and asking to borrow money, or who was having legal issues. And those things certainly wouldn't have been repeated to the person who was the topic of discussion. But if someone took things too far or spoke out of turn, someone else would say, "Okay now, mind yo' business," and everyone knew to change the subject.

Culture and social history have given what some people see as unspoken permission to pry, poke, impose, and project onto other people's lives. But I find that involving yourself in what others have going on is also the reason many families and friends experience unhealthy discourse and broken relationships. When we get involved in other people's business, we cross their boundaries and invite them to cross ours.

STAYING IN YOUR POWER

One of the most common ways people relinquish their power is by focusing their energy on things they can't change. When you are in your power, you are focused on things that matter to you, you are fully present to the moment you are in, you are living true to yourself, and you are honoring your own purpose, values, and personal abilities. Anything you can't control is outside of your power.

I think you know this. Your experience proves it. But think back on the times you tried to change someone. How did that work out for you? Consider the times you gave unsolicited advice to a friend or family member. How did those conversations end? Remember when you wanted something for someone more than they wanted it for themselves? Who ended up being disappointed and dismayed?

Minding your business is not a practice of abandoning the ones you love. It's a habit of not abandoning your own peace by trying to control people or even things you don't have the ability to control.

Things You Can't Control

- What someone thinks about you. That is none of your business.

- If someone values you. That is none of your business.

- Someone else's lifestyle. That is none of your business.

- Someone else's preferences. That is none of your business.

- When/if someone changes. That is none of your business.

- Someone else's mindset or beliefs. That is none of your business.

- Whom someone chooses to love. That is none of your business.

Focusing on things you *can* control is how you stay in your power. Minding your own business is how you protect your peace and secure your healing.

WHY MINDING YOUR OWN BUSINESS MATTERS

My friend Heather had been in an abusive marriage for twenty years when we met. It got physical—often—and now she felt like her husband was turning her children against her. He was starting to question her parenting in front of them and shower them with gifts instead of holding them accountable for poor grades or evading chores. In a matter of weeks, she went from bubbly, driven, and inspired, to appearing unmotivated and distant.

It was difficult to see someone I cared about show up with bruises on her neck and arms. (She tried covering it up, but it was apparent.) We connected as friends, so I tried hard to honor a boundary I set to keep my professional opinions to myself, and just be the friend. As her friend, I would listen and cry with her, and give advice only when she asked. I encouraged her to pursue her goal of completing her doctorate degree and to accept requests for speaking engagements, and I reminded her of how valuable she was as a friend, mother, and professional.

There was an interesting pattern in Heather's and my friendship. After reaching a breaking point, she would ask me for help with resources, and I would connect her with advocates, housing options, and legal assistance. She would seem hopeful and take the help, only to get right back with her husband days later. I remember feeling frustrated and emotionally drained. But as Heather's friend, I thought my duty was to be there for her, no matter what.

I had come to define being there for her as

- Getting her access to the help she needed (even if she didn't take it)

- Nursing her back to health when she was bruised and battered

- Listening to her vent or unload her emotions about her relationship

- Treating her like a friend and not a client

Ultimately, my friendship with Heather became emotionally exhausting and triggered thoughts of traumatic experiences from my own life. I wanted to save her, just as I had tried (and failed) to save some of my closest family members. But, having worked as a program director of a domestic violence advocacy center and shelter, I knew that it could take up to seven attempts for a survivor to finally release/escape an abusive relationship. This cycle Heather was stuck in was not uncommon. I was doing everything I could, but at some point I had to acknowledge my limits.

This situation helped me realize that I had developed a pattern of consuming myself with the business of those I loved. As a family member or friend, I felt obligated to facilitate their healing, to help reprogram their patterns, and to push, pull, or drag them into what I thought was best for them. This level of codependency took a toll on my own well-being. I started to lose hair, lose energy, and lose myself in their lives.

There are times when being in someone else's business soothes our own trauma. We see someone else feeling the same pain, and it gives us a sense of "me too." Or we show up for others, and perhaps it makes us feel valued and needed after years of feeling unworthy and of no use. If we aren't careful, we can become enmeshed with the people we are trying to support, to the point where we no longer see the distinction between their lives and our own.

I knew I needed to take a step back and save myself. So I gave Heather one last pep talk and a folder full of all the resources I had. Then I released her to herself. I didn't cut our friendship off completely, but I did set a boundary for myself not to engage her in conversations about her marriage or the abuse. I think Heather realized how her issues were impacting me emotionally, and in response, she chose to distance herself. When she was ready, more than two years later, she left her husband for good. She now works as an advocate for other survivors. That experience led me to these lessons in minding your own business:

- You cannot determine what's best for someone else. Everyone has their own perspective, values, beliefs, and preferences.

- You can't expect someone to do for you what they are unwilling to do for themselves. Change requires the agreement and participation of the person who needs it.

- When you interfere with someone living their own life, you interfere with their ability to learn their own lessons.

- There is freedom in allowing people to be who they are, live how they want, and change when or if they are ready. They are free to live their lives and you are free to live yours.

THE DIFFERENCE BETWEEN EMPOWERING AND ENABLING

While you can't heal, change, or grow other people, you can support their own efforts to do so. Part of the work of minding your own business is knowing the difference between empowering your loved ones and enabling them.

So far, we've talked about how *we* tend to cross the line into other people's business. But even when people extend invitations to involve us in their lives, there are times when it's in our best interest to decline.

Sometimes, people expect others to do what they don't want to do themselves. They want you to confront the bully in their life, they want you to help pay their bills, they want you to give them permission to leave the toxic relationship, and they need you to bear the responsibility of keeping them from harmful behaviors like addiction. They often pull on the heartstrings of a helper to intervene, and the intervention prevents them from building up their own agency.

This dynamic can be found in relationships between a parent and an adult child, a loved one and a person with an addiction, a victim and an abuser, a codependent partner and a narcissistic one, or a friend in a one-sided relationship with another person.

You may not mean to contribute to your loved ones' poor decisions, lack of accountability, or negative habits. But when you engage in their lives by doing things on their behalf or making excuses for the things that don't get done at all, you are aiding and abetting their self-sabotage. You don't have to mind someone's business to show you love and care for them. You can love them by setting them up with enough words of encouragement, and sometimes even resources, that lead to their handling their own business.

You will know you've crossed the line between empowering and enabling when

- *You start covering or downplaying a person's negative actions*
- *You try loving someone out of their problems*
- *You make excuses for unchanged behavior*
- *You take responsibility for someone else's actions*
- *You break promises to yourself not to intervene*
- *You tolerate toxic, abusive, or destructive behavior*
- *You deny the severity of someone's circumstance to prevent them from feeling bad*

The person you are enabling might be known among your family or friend group as the one who is always messing up, falling off, and needing to be bailed out. That's because no one has given them the freedom they need to finally get things right. If you stop giving your cousin help with his rent money, he may be forced to take extra hours at work to come up with the money himself. If you stop positioning yourself in the middle of a disagreement between your other siblings, they may learn to talk to each other directly and come to a peaceful resolution. You will be surprised by what people can do when they have no other choice. You will be surprised how consistent, intentional, and strategic someone can be when no one else is around to be those things for them.

WHAT MINDING OUR OWN BUSINESS HEALS IN US

As with most of the habits in this book, I have to be intentional about minding my own business. I am a helper by nature. I care deeply about the success, growth, and healing of everyone in my life. My chosen roles—consultant, educator, mentor, facilitator of healing—all require me to ask personal questions and discern insights into the lives of others. In my professional and personal lives, I've had to learn when to lean in and be supportive, and when to fall back.

Before getting into someone else's business, I've learned to ask

- Did they ask for my help, advice, or support?

- What are my intentions for getting involved?

- How will getting involved impact me personally?

- Is this person/situation my personal responsibility?

- Do I have the mental, physical, or financial capacity to help?

- Am I willing to bear the consequences of the outcome of this situation?

- Will getting involved make things better or make me bitter?

- Will getting involved empower the other person or enable them?

Consider how being a helper makes *you* feel. Does watching someone take your advice validate your need to be heard? Does coming to someone else's rescue actually rescue a prior version of yourself who needed the same intervention? Does judging, gossiping, or projecting help you hide the ways you do the things you are so quick to point out in someone else's life?

Minding your own business heals your relationship with your energy. It helps you see that your wisdom to solve problems and talent for making things happen for others can be used to do the same things in your *own* life. We spend a lot of our energy trying to heal ourselves by helping other people. Instead, we should go straight to the source—focusing that attention, care, and encouragement and applying it to our own lives. Reserve those powerful things for yourself until you are invited to share them with others. Allow others the freedom to transform their own futures by tapping into their own gifts, talents, skills, and experiences to increase their own agency and build meaningful lives.

MINDING YOUR OWN BUSINESS AND RECLAIMING YOUR POWER

Your energy is your power to sustain mental and physical effort. Scientists define energy as the ability to do work. So minding your own business does more than just call your focus back to yourself; it helps you reclaim your power by ensuring that you have enough of the mental and physical stamina needed to do powerful work in your own life.

I said earlier that you will be amazed by what other people can do when you aren't doing everything for them. And that's true. You will also be amazed by what you can do for yourself when all your energy isn't spent doing things for others.

Reclaiming your power looks like strengthening your gifts, talents, and skills and leveraging them in a new business venture. It looks like cultivating relationship wisdom and using it to create a new legacy of healing in your own family. It looks like better managing your time during the day so you can fit in your daily self-care habits. The habit of minding your business guarantees that you have the power to meet your own needs and heal your own life.

SEVEN STEPS TO BEGIN MINDING YOUR OWN BUSINESS

1. **Accept people as they are and choose wisely who you want to keep in your circle.** A part of minding your business is not trying to change someone, not trying to act on someone's behalf, and being certain that the people in your life are aligned with your values and standards for connection.

2. **Avoid gossip and harsh judgments.** Remember that not everyone shares the same worldview. Gossiping and judging are projections. Minding your own business protects your view and the views of others.

3. **Be responsible for your own thoughts and feelings.** Other people's thoughts and feelings are not your responsibility to manage or uphold. And even when what someone else says or thinks about you is hurtful to you, you are empowered to work through the hurt and respond in ways that protect your heart and your peace.

4. **Keep your unsolicited opinions to yourself.** Just because you think something doesn't mean you have to say it. This is true unless someone asks you—but I would qual-

ify that by adding that *if* what you have to say in response isn't meaningful, mind your own business.

5. **Regulate your emotions.** Often, we are moved to pry, gossip, or enable because of our own unresolved emotions. Pause and examine the root of what you're feeling before you decide to respond with your emotions and get in someone else's business. This pause will help you determine if you genuinely want to be invested for the sake of others, or to soothe your unhealed feelings.

6. **Follow the rule of "Me, Us, or We."** This one is simple: If the business isn't about me, us, or we, it's not mine. "Me" is yourself, "us" could be your immediate family members or close friends that could be impacted, and "we" is you and the other people directly involved—for instance, you and a sibling, co-worker, or friend. This is a great rule because it invites you to focus on things that matter and things that you can control.

7. **Establish boundaries.** We will explore boundaries more in the next chapter, but for now, it's worth considering what it means to have clear guidelines for getting involved in someone else's life. The boundary may be "I share my thoughts on my sister's marriage only if she asks me" or "I'll help out financially only one time a year, and only if they can come up with 50 percent of their need" or "I will avoid gossip at work by eating lunch in my office." Minding other people's business is a huge energy drain. Boundaries will prevent the deficit.

PROMPTS FOR MINDING
YOUR OWN BUSINESS

In what areas of your life do you need to practice minding your own business? Whose life are you preoccupied with? Did they ask for your opinion, help, or support? If they asked, is it because they aren't taking responsibility for their own life?

Why do you need to mind your own business? Will you have more time and energy to focus on your own life? Will it help break the cycle of enabling others? Will minding your own business empower you and the people you love?

What does minding your own business look like? Will you help only those who ask? Will you stop enabling specific family members? Will you set a boundary that separates you as a professional from you as a family member or friend?

How will you practice the habit of minding your own business today, this week, and/or this month? What are the actions you can commit to doing? Can you recommit your focus to your own life? Can you start or finish a personal project you've been neglecting? Can you seek therapy to address your need to save others?

USE THE SPACE BELOW TO WORK
THROUGH THE PROMPTS ON YOUR OWN

Need: _____

_____

_____

Why do I need to do this? _____

_____

_____

Healing Habits: _____

_____

_____

Practices/Action: _____

_____

_____

AFFIRMATIONS FOR
MINDING YOUR OWN BUSINESS

Say this out loud with me:

I mind the business that belongs to me.
My life deserves my attention and energy.
I reserve my insights for those who ask.
I give other people the freedom to show up for themselves.
I use my wisdom, talents, and skills to improve my
    own life.

Chapter 8

THE HABIT OF CONFRONTATION: HOW SETTING BOUNDARIES HEALS OUR RELATIONSHIP WITH CONNECTION

During seasons when my grandmom was particularly overwhelmed, I stayed on my best behavior. The stress of working multiple jobs, raising a bonus child, and living in a home with people who were struggling with drug use made her easily angered. I was only seven or eight then, but I didn't want to add to her troubles by misbehaving at school or around the house.

When I would slip and make age-appropriate mistakes, like not being truthful about the candy I ate, staying outside after the streetlights came on, or getting notes sent home from my teacher for talking too much in class, my grandmom would discipline me with a lecture and a whupping. She would also tag this one sentence at the end of some of her lectures: ". . . and you can go stay with your mom, because I am too old and too tired for this."

That one sentence hurt worse than getting hit with her belt. It validated every negative thing I believed about myself at the time. I was a burden. I was optional. I wasn't a choice. I was too much.

She would say it only when everything else in her life was extremely tough, but those words hurt me deeply. As I sat on the edge of the bed in my room, I remember thinking, *Why did you take me in at all?*

One day when I was a few years older, I had gotten in trouble for another minor slip. I can't remember what I did, but I know it wasn't something that warranted the punishment I was going to receive. This time, when my grandmom threw that one sentence at me, I remember saying a short and silent prayer for the courage (and protection from that belt) to voice what I would normally only think to myself. I looked my grandmom in the eye, and cautiously said, "Why did you take me in?"

She stopped in her tracks. My question seemed to confuse her. Her gaze wasn't threatening. It was stoic at first, and then morphed into a look of remorse. Despite my fear (and, yeah, I was scared as hell), I repeated my question, adding words I will never forget. I said, "If you are too old and too tired for me, why did you take me in? I am not a bad kid. I try as hard as I can not to be . . . I don't make you worry or cry like your sons, I'm not in the streets, I'm not pregnant, and I'm not on drugs. When you're stressed, you say things to me that hurt me worse than the belt. Maybe I should leave so I'm not another person stressing you out."

There was silence. Thinking back, it felt like forever, but it was probably more like a minute or so. I braced myself on the edge of the bed, preparing for the worst. But instead, my grandmom walked over to me and gave me a hug. When she released her hold, she had tears in her eyes. She apologized for her words and promised she'd never say them again. And she didn't. Ever.

That moment taught me that everyone has limits, and if we don't share those limits with the people in our lives, they will continue to push them. It was my first real lesson on boundaries. The courage I gained from having that talk has never left me. A precedent was set. I discovered that I could protect my heart, my peace, my values, and the relationships that matter to me.

I also learned that my grandmom, flaws and all, was one of the most amazing people in my world. In that moment, she embodied the healing habits we've discussed in this book. She showed empathy. and was accepting. She let go of antiquated ways of parenting and allowed me to use my voice and express my heart. She held herself accountable for changing and forgiving herself. She held space for my perspective and didn't take it personally. That one conversation changed the dynamic of our entire relationship.

MY DEFINITION OF BOUNDARIES

Boundaries are a specific set of standards, needs, and limits that help support your well-being and help you feel comfortable in your relationship with others. Although setting boundaries with others may feel easier when the people you are setting them for cooperate, it's your responsibility to set them. You can make requests of other people, offer suggestions, and share your needs, but ultimately honoring a boundary is something that requires action. Developing the habit of saying "no" when you need to say it, asking for help, for space, or for clarity when you need it, and expressing your feelings, concerns, or expectations when they arise is essential to the health and well-being of your relationships.

RESISTANCE TO SETTING BOUNDARIES

Setting boundaries is something you get better at with practice. If you wait until you and a family member are at odds with each other, until you and your co-worker are behind on a project, or until you and your partner are rethinking your commitment to each other, setting boundaries will become something you fear instead of something you can confidently face.

Our history with boundaries determines how we impose and

accept them. If your family tended to ignore limits, invade each other's spaces, downplay each other's needs, or disregard what each other said, you might have grown up lacking the skills needed to identify, communicate, and honor healthy boundaries as an adult. You may fear being assertive about your needs and you may have trouble accepting when other people are being assertive about their own.

HOW FAMILIAL HISTORY IMPACTS OUR RESISTANCE TO BOUNDARIES

I come from a children-are-seen-and-not-heard kind of family. I had very little say over my life. My bedroom door was expected to stay open at all times, my phone conversations with friends took place in the living room surrounded by everyone who was home at the time, and no one had their own any-thing. Food, clothing, jewelry, money, toiletries, and other things I now deem as *mine* were *ours* as far as my family was concerned. There was no such thing as limits, standards, or needs that were my own, so I had every reason to fear hav-ing that tough conversation with my grandmom about how her words were affecting me.

> *You may be afraid to assert a boundary when*
>
> - *Setting a boundary may highlight how you are different from the people in your life, making you feel alienated*
> - *Your boundaries were judged or rejected in the past*
> - *A relationship ended when you set a boundary in the past*
> - *You are uncertain how someone will respond to your boundaries*
> - *You want to please and be accepted by others*
> - *You don't know how to communicate your needs*

Whenever I speak, facilitate a workshop, or host a session with clients on the subject of boundaries, I always go back to that conversation with my grandmom. Years ago, I asked for her blessing to share it publicly because it was such a defining moment in my relationship with her and with boundaries. Being brave and vulnerable enough to confront my grandmom with a boundary, and having her response be one of empathy and respect, impacted how I would set boundaries in the future.

Take a moment and consider your earliest experiences with boundaries:

- Could you share your feelings with a parent or parental figure without fear of punishment?

- Were you allowed to say "no," have privacy in your own space, or speak up in defense of yourself as a child?

- Were you encouraged to have a perspective that was different from everyone else's? Or were you criticized whenever you took a different stance than the family?

It is natural to fear doing something that could negatively impact your relationships. Your needs may conflict with the needs of others. Your limits may change the dynamic of how you engage with some of the most important people in your life. A difficult conversation may determine if someone stays or goes. But the hard truth is that you may *never* feel comfortable setting a boundary that you absolutely need to set. The price of peace, joy in your relationships, feeling seen and heard, and ultimately having your needs met might not be a small one, but it's worth every bit of the courage it takes to do it.

HOW TRAUMA HISTORY IMPACTS OUR RESISTANCE TO BOUNDARIES

In addition to family history, trauma history also affects the way we set and receive boundaries. For example, abuse in and of itself is a violation of boundaries. There is an unspoken expectation that your physical, emotional, sexual, and spiritual needs will be protected in close relationships, but that unspoken agreement changes when those areas are breached by those we love. The secrecy that often accompanies abuse, the silencing that often comes with disclosing it, and the guilt and shame that are a result of the stigma attached to it all play a part in how or *if* we communicate a boundary.

I understand that all of this and any other instance of trauma in your history can perpetuate fear of advocating for yourself in the future. But I want you to take a moment to pause and try to see past your fear: Imagine how it would feel to experience a new level of power over your life.

SIX SIGNS YOU NEED TO SET BOUNDARIES

1. **You will know you need to set boundaries when you start feeling resentful and bitter.** In relationships that lack boundaries, people often feel frustrated, irritated, and annoyed. You might feel this way if you go out of your way to support others but feel emotionally depleted because that same support and energy is not reciprocated. This pattern can build up to feelings of long-term resentment. If you're starting to feel bitterness in your relationships, try communicating the support you need.

2. **You will know you need to set boundaries when you start betraying your own heart.** When you are doing things out of obligation instead of inspiration, when you say "yes" to things you'd rather say "no" to, or when you do things that go against your own standards and values—you are betraying your own needs. Honoring your boundaries is how you honor your heart. Sometimes you have to challenge your actions to ensure they are aligned with what you need and want.

3. **You will know you need to set boundaries when you tolerate toxic behavior or abuse.** There should be no place in your life for behavior that chips away at the health of your heart, causes you to question your worth, or threatens your physical, mental, and emotional well-being. Even when a person isn't intentionally trying to cause harm, their words and actions have a negative impact. Sharing your physical and emotional limits in your relationships makes being in connection with others safe.

4. **You will know you need to set boundaries when you are afraid to speak up for yourself.** When you fear being honest, asking for help, expressing a concern, or sharing what you want or need in your relationships, you lack emotional safety and comfort. Hiding or shrinking any part of you, in your relationship, means you are showing up in pieces when you deserve to be whole. Boundaries will give you the freedom to show up fully as yourself.

5. **You will know you need to set boundaries when your relationship tends to be difficult and filled with drama.** When there are constant arguments, avoidant behavior

(ignoring, disappearing, shutting down, or cutting each other off), and immature plays for power or control, these are signs that the relationship lacks standards, limits, and clear expectations. That kind of emotional labor isn't good for your connection or your health. Chaos isn't cute and it doesn't spice things up in your relationship; it's toxic.

6. **You will know you need to set boundaries when you lose your sense of self.** When your entire identity is tied to the role you play in the lives of other people, it can be a sign that you lack self-care, self-awareness, and ultimately self-actualization. You will relate to this issue if your entire calendar, outside of work, is filled with things you do for others, like dinners, showing up for sporting events, caretaking, or being their emotional support person. If you have free time, you may have no idea what to do with it because you are so used to using it for others.

WHAT SETTING BOUNDARIES WITH FAMILY LOOKS LIKE

I had a conversation with my client Elise a few days after she had asked her father and sister to pack up and leave her home, during a visit. You heard that right. She kicked her own father (and sister) out of her house. She felt they were rude and had violated one of the rules of her home, so she said it was time for them to leave. And they did.

Elise told me that she shared this experience with her friend and they said her actions were mean. When we discussed it, I said it meant she had boundaries. While I was talking, Elise googled the definition of boundary; although she had been enacting them for years, she had no idea it was a legit thing. I explained to Elise that she did well by expressing her expectations to her father and sister, but they had dismissed her feelings. I was proud of her, because once she started to feel resentment rising, she took responsibility for her own needs and created the space she needed to process her feelings and prevent further damage to her relationships. Elise's father and sister didn't want to suffer the consequences either, so they left without resistance. Their relationships remain intact to this day.

Of course, it doesn't always go that way. Most of the people I've worked with describe setting boundaries with family as the hardest habit to create. They didn't want to hurt their mother-in-law's or parents' feelings by asking them to call to find out if it was a convenient time before coming over to visit. They were met with resistance when explaining to a sibling that their personal relationship was off-limits after deciding to work things out with a partner.

Our families are our first experience in relationships, which means they're the perfect place to start building our boundary muscle. The experience of erecting a boundary with a sibling may make it easier to do so later on with a co-worker. Asking a parent for what you need to feel seen in the family may be good practice before asking a boss for a raise. Remember, you may never feel completely comfortable with setting a boundary, but you can grow to do it with more ease.

Fair warning: If you begin setting boundaries, some people might misinterpret your behavior as meanness. A family member who had issues with substance use and money once called me mean for not buying them alcohol and cigarettes. One of my aunts gave me the nickname Miss Missy (that I actually loved) for being assertive about what I didn't want to eat, didn't want to wear, and where I didn't want to go as a child.

Some of those actions changed my relationship with the people involved. Still, I wasn't being mean. I identified a need, a standard, a more sustainable way of being, and I honored that—even when it made others uncomfortable. I was doing something else most people miss: I set boundaries that were created to protect myself *and* preserve the relationship.

Setting a boundary says, "I want to stay in relationship with you and this boundary is what I need to feel safe and comfortable enough to do that." I actually start my conversations around boundaries that way:

"*I appreciate our relationship so much.*"

"*Family is at the top of my list of values.*"

"*I don't want our love for each other to be negatively impacted.*"

"*I respect you and want to protect our relationship.*"

> *Boundaries with family members may look like*
>
> - *Taking discussions about your personal relationship off the table*
> - *Giving rules about acceptable behavior at your house*
> - *Not attending family dinner when you don't have the capacity to*
> - *Not allowing others to discipline your children*
> - *Asking a disrespectful relative to leave your home*
> - *Not picking a side when other family members are in a disagreement*
> - *Having close relationships with friends without including a sibling or cousin*

It may take several conversations. It will take a period of adjustment. You may have to honor a boundary from someone else in response to your own. But boundaries preserve relationships by ensuring that everyone involved is protected. This was the case for my family members who were on the receiving end of some of my boundaries. Although they had to adjust, they appreciated the fact that I communicated my needs and limits, and that I chose to do that instead of cutting them off.

WHAT SETTING BOUNDARIES WITH A PARTNER LOOKS LIKE

When you are done with someone, the boundary is distance. When you want to save or maintain a relationship, the boundary is changed behavior. Habits that protect your boundaries look like direct communication, creating a schedule, assigning chores around the house, and having physical space. These types of habits preserve our most valued relationships, so deciding to opt for a boundary over a breakup is a major step toward relationship repair.

Relationships that lack boundaries are breeding grounds for arguments, misunderstandings, and other conflicts that can lead to emotional and physical distance. A healthy relationship is a series of choices and behaviors.

Here are some boundary choices you should consider if you're in a romantic relationship

- *Set standards concerning fidelity.*
- *Have the money talk (financial status, goals, responsibilities, spending habits).*
- *Decide how to handle disputes over things like purchases, parenting, or household matters.*
- *Share your independent needs, goals, and desires.*
- *Discuss parenting desires, options, and expectations (when or if you want children, and how you would raise them).*
- *Decide how much access to give outsiders (friends and family).*
- *Tell each other your deal-breakers.*

No one ends up in their idea of a perfect relationship by accident. Partners intent on building a perfect relationship incorporate honest conversations, clear standards, agreed-upon expectations, and established boundaries.

WHY BOUNDARIES MATTER

Boundaries are set in relationships with people you want to stay connected to. When you reframe boundaries with this specific intent in mind, it sheds a whole new light on them. It puts into perspective how specific actions can contribute to the health of your relationship with your loved ones. It makes standards and expectations known to prevent ambiguity and unintentional harm. Sharing your needs with someone is an act of vulnerability—and we are vulnerable with those we love and trust. To feel safe, supported, and deeply con-

You need boundaries in your relationships to

- *Meet your needs and the needs of the other person*
- *Communicate clear and reasonable expectations*
- *Express limits and/or desires for expansion and growth*
- *Avoid toxic behaviors*
- *Minimize negative emotions like resentment and bitterness*
- *Stay mentally and emotionally well*

nected to our loved ones, we need to share the ways they can honor our needs—a need that goes both ways. You should create a safe space for your loved ones to share their boundaries with you as well.

The earlier in the relationship you create a habit of setting boundaries, the better. Establish agreements about who is responsible for paying specific bills, taking out the trash, responding to the mail, and cleaning up the kitchen after dinner. Sync relationship expectations about how often to go out for date night or spend time with friends, how much time you need alone to decompress, and whether exchanging gifts for special occasions is one of the ways you will show love.

Outline relationship standards that account for each person's mental, emotional, and physical capacity, as well as your individual values. Think of these as preventative habits. *Relationship boundaries can prevent a lot of misunderstandings. And if a positive relationship that lacks boundaries finds itself in trouble down the line, boundaries are also great for repairing relationships.* If your relationships are suffering because you don't have clear boundaries in place, it's not too late to repair the damage. Start to identify your needs and begin to set boundaries, immediately.

It's also possible to have good boundaries in one area of your relationship but not in another. Maybe you have good boundaries in place at home and in your marriage, but you need boundaries with extended family members. Maybe you are clear on who takes out the trash and who cleans up the kitchen, but not on who initiates dates and intimacy. *The need for setting boundaries never expires.* As you grow as individuals, and in love, so does your need for boundaries. It is naïve to think that the person you get into a relationship with stays the same forever, so as we evolve our boundaries can too.

People are supposed to change. And as they change, so will their specific need for boundaries. Perhaps revisit your boundaries after every major life change, or even yearly—during your anniversary month. And of course, have the conversation around boundaries whenever an immediate need to do so arises. You are not expected to be your partner's therapist, but you can tell when something may be off with them personally, or in the relationship. You can do this by simply asking, "You seem tense. Is there anything I can do to help?" or "How can I help out around the house while you are working on your project?" Essentially you are asking, "Is there a boundary I can honor for you?"

WHAT SETTING BOUNDARIES HEALS IN US

A relationship is the most vulnerable place to be. Connecting with others in any kind of relationship requires an open heart, mind, and spirit. Setting boundaries creates safety, which fosters genuine connection.

You need family members who give you the space to be yourself. You need friends who don't disclose your secrets. You need a partner who supports your efforts. Boundaries make those needs clear and protect you against violations of your vulnerability.

A hard truth that may be difficult to hear is that the people who will have the most trouble with your boundaries are the ones who want to cross them. Someone resisting your habit of doing what's best for you is the real problem, not your boundaries.

Asking for what you need to feel safe and supported will expose who is for you and who isn't. So instead of experiencing relationships where your limits are pushed or you feel disrespected, expressing your boundaries will reveal people's true character, thereby helping you choose safer, more aligned connections instead.

A life without boundaries is a life without peace. You pay in peace when a lack of boundaries allows burnout, anxiousness, discontentment, frustration, and resentment to seep into your life. You pay in peace when your relationships are unpredictable, contemptuous, abusive, exhausting, and lack reciprocation. You pay in peace when you are not in control of your finances, time, safety, career, and emotions.

Setting boundaries is how you secure your peace, but it is also how you reclaim your power.

SETTING BOUNDARIES TO RECLAIM
YOUR POWER

I can always tell when a client is happy in their relationships. Their updates are filled with stories of quality time connecting with others and instances where someone showed up for them with support and encouragement. They are also prone to spontaneous self-improvement like taking risks, applying for jobs, or moving to a new state. They are proud to share regular wins like getting in better shape, or the promising early success of their new business. One client bragged about gaining what she called happy weight while falling in love because, hey, a win is a win.

The quality of your relationships determines the quality of your life. When you have healthy boundaries in your relationships you tend to be less anxious, tense, and distracted by petty quarrels. These boundaries create the emotional space for joy, focus, and dreaming up ideas to improve your life. Loving, reciprocal, safe, and supportive relationships contribute positively to our well-being. We experience those relationship qualities by setting the boundaries that create space for them. We reclaim our power when we cultivate healthy relationships. We thrive in life when we are seen, heard, felt, and loved well.

The habit of setting boundaries ultimately empowers you to get your needs met. Instead of hoping someone will accurately guess what you want and need, you get to ask for it directly.

THREE STEPS TO BEGIN SETTING
BOUNDARIES

To set a boundary with yourself or others, you must do three things: Identify a need, decide on an action, and communicate the boundary.

1. **Identify a need.** A recurring question throughout this book has been *What do I need?* What are some specific standards, needs, and limits that help support your well-being and help you feel comfortable in your relationships (including the one you have with yourself)? Identifying the specific need creates awareness, and being aware of your needs empowers you to meet them.

   It's important to note here that your need could be to heal childhood trauma, move forward after a divorce, or feel safe after an assault. Your need can be physical, emotional, or related to your mental health. Boundaries are part of the process, no matter what healing journey you are on.

2. **Decide on an action.** A boundary is an action word. You do not have a boundary unless an action is assigned to it. "I'm tired of doing everything myself" is not a boundary. "You always come over unannounced" is not a boundary. "I don't appreciate everyone giving opinions on my marriage" is not a boundary. There should be action directed toward your need, and it shouldn't be totally dependent on the participation of someone else. You can make requests and suggestions that include the people you are in a relationship with, but to ensure that your needs are met, you must be willing to take the action yourself.

   If you need more time to yourself, you might consider asking your spouse or partner to assist you by taking responsibility for your shared children. But you still need to identify the action you will take if they say "no." You may have to enlist the help of another family member, pay for a babysitter yourself, or wake up earlier in the morning to have time alone. After you've decided the action you are willing to take if your spouse is unable or unwilling to help out, try talking through your expectations of the experience and the responsibilities you need to prioritize.

It's essential to take this action in your boundaries with yourself too. The action might look like leaving work at your designated end time, saying "no" to babysitting your niece when you are not up to it, asking someone to pronounce your name correctly, or asking to have your morning coffee remade if the order was incorrect.

3. **Communicate the boundary.** *If it's not said, it's not seen.* People cannot read your mind. Sighs, moans, shoulder shrugs, and eye rolls are not mature forms of communication. To set a boundary, you must be direct in the way you communicate the action needed. "I wish you wouldn't speak to me that way" is not a boundary. "I will not continue this conversation with you if you continue to speak to me that way" is a boundary. And make sure that once you've voiced the boundary, you are prepared to follow through with the consequential action.

HERE ARE SOME
POWERFUL TRUTHS TO REMEMBER

- You are responsible for your own boundaries.

- You may never feel totally comfortable setting a boundary, but you can learn to do it with more ease.

- Waiting to set a boundary until there is a problem can create more problems.

- You may have to give the people in your life some time to adjust to new boundaries.

- When you honor your boundaries, so will everyone else (even if honoring them looks like agreeing or accepting that the relationship needs to end).

- You can't get mad at someone for crossing a boundary you never set.

PROMPTS FOR SETTING BOUNDARIES

In what areas of your life do you need to establish a boundary? Where do you struggle to say "no"? Is there a family member who keeps testing your limits? Are you experiencing burnout? Do you need to set limits with yourself?

Why do you need to set a boundary? Will setting a boundary improve your relationship with your spouse or partner? Will setting a boundary improve your health? Will financial boundaries help you meet a specific goal?

What does setting boundaries look like? Will you not answer a call from an emotionally abusive relative? Will you have a money or parenting talk with a spouse or partner? Will you ask for time off from your job?

How will you practice the habit of setting boundaries today, this week, and/or this month? What are the actions you can commit to doing? Can you create a family schedule that includes your alone time, hours you will be available for helping others, and times you will request help from someone else? Will you say "no" to lending money to a friend?

USE THE SPACE BELOW TO WORK
THROUGH THE PROMPTS ON YOUR OWN

Need: _____

_____

_____

Why do I need to do this? _____

_____

_____

Healing Habits: _____

_____

_____

Practices/Action: _____

_____

_____

AFFIRMATIONS FOR
SETTING BOUNDARIES

Say this out loud with me:

I am allowed to say "no" to things I don't have the capacity
for.
I will respect my limits.
I will use my voice to state my needs.
The more I practice enforcing my boundaries, the easier it
will be.
My boundaries keep me safe and supported.

Chapter 9

THE HABIT OF NOT SETTLING: HOW REMEMBERING WHO YOU ARE HEALS YOUR RELATIONSHIP WITH POSSIBILITY

I have been an encourager of sorts for as long as I can remember. I encouraged my parents, my friends' parents, and even my fourth-grade teacher, Ms. Vee.

Within the first couple of weeks of school, Ms. Vee moved my desk right next to hers. Her plan was to keep me away from distractions, since I tended to talk a lot in class. Within two weeks, we had gotten close. I had gained the unofficial title of her "student therapist."

While other students used their free time to play and talk among themselves, I listened to Ms. Vee share her relationship woes. She was in her mid-twenties and discouraged because she didn't have a lot of dating prospects. The few dates I remember us talking about were arranged by her friends and never turned into something serious. As Ms. Vee confided in me, I was somehow able to encourage her not to settle in her dating relationships, not to appear desperate, and not to allow her family to project their beliefs onto her. At just nine years old, I know I didn't use those exact words, but looking back, those were the messages that always seemed to get through.

There is one conversation I will always remember from one of our unofficial sessions. Ms. Vee's brother, who was married with kids, had just purchased a beautiful home with a pool in the backyard. I remember driving by that house many times as a kid, staring in admiration. It was the literal "house with a white picket fence" everyone dreamed of owning one day. From our talks, I knew that Ms. Vee dreamed of that. She wanted the house, the white picket fence, the marriage, and the babies. But at that moment, all she had was herself and her students.

On that particular day, Ms. Vee was venting about how her current situation wasn't good enough for her parents because they thought she should have been married by then. Ms. Vee was a heavier woman who always made fun of her weight and her self-described "bushy Italian eyebrows." She said that her parents were also constantly criticizing her appearance, as well as the area she lived and worked in. Now she was wondering if these perceived flaws were the reason she was still single.

So, I leaned across my desk to get closer to hers, looked up from my classwork, and said something that only a nine-year-old could pull off: "Ms. Vee, if your parents think you're ugly, they must be ugly too because kids look like their parents." She laughed out loud. I added, "The next time they make you feel ugly, tell them what I said."

Ms. Vee was an excellent teacher. She made learning fun and accessible. She was firm and effective, empathetic and inspiring. But the pressure Ms. Vee's family put on her to get married and have children made her forget that her mission to help at-risk youth like me was *just* as valuable. Their projections, opinions, and criticism created a narrative that made her feel as if she wasn't good enough—and she started to mistake it for the truth.

After leaving school, I kept in touch with Ms. Vee for a few years. She needed to know that her work was in fact as valuable as she thought it was, and that I was a living, breathing record of her success.

The version of me that counseled my fourth-grade teacher has grown into the person I am today. Whenever I'm questioning my effectiveness or feeling like an impostor, I look back and remember that the wisdom and kindness I displayed at nine years old is still inside my soul. I have always been me.

Buried under the circumstances, the disappointments, the failed relationships, and the painful parts of your life is a version of you that has always existed. You may have some digging to do, but if you take some time to yourself, you'll remember the helper you were in kindergarten, the dreamer you were in fifth grade, the wise sage who kept your friends out of trouble at sixteen, the negotiator who won the argument with your parents over your curfew, the financial wizard who saved enough money to buy your first car, the advocate who got the housing rules amended in college, the giver who never passed a homeless person without helping, and the highest version of you who still seeks ways to heal and grow.

Before we dive deeper into this lesson, I want you to pause for a few seconds and hold space for the reflections that have already come to mind as you begin to remember who you are. Buried inside these memories, you'll see how selflessness, dreaming, wisdom, intelligence, and so many more things are already a part of your identity. All those beautiful things that you are striving to be have always been inside you.

WHAT IT MEANS TO REMEMBER
WHO YOU ARE

Remembering who you are is more than reflecting on memories from your past. It is the never-ending practice of anchoring yourself in the ideas, values, gifts, purpose, and calling that are unique to you. This anchoring is essential, because when life pulls you in different directions or people project their views onto you, you can always find your way back to the truth of who you are.

Everything that you've experienced, good or bad, has contributed to the moment you are in right now. Those experiences have informed your beliefs, guided your choices, cultivated your values, inspired your standards, and developed your habits.

The people who shared those experiences with you have also informed and inspired who you've become, but ultimately *you* have decided how you want to show up in the world. That decision may not have been easy. It can be difficult to manage the sum of both the good and the bad experiences that make us who we are. At times, you may find yourself struggling to handle current circumstances, shifting back and forth between your past automatic responses and the new, healthier responses inspired by your healing journey.

If you are not careful, life will happen *to* you and slowly begin to strip you of the truth of who you are. You'll start to believe in the opinions of others. You'll rely too much on their validation. You'll do what other people want you to do, and the narratives that other people create about you will become the story of your life.

When you *are* careful, life will feel like it's happening *for* you. Every experience will be a piece of information that helps you decide who you want to be. You'll see opinions as options and not facts. You'll see validation as something you give to yourself because you are in the habit of not taking things personally. Other people's priorities won't trump what *you* want to do, and the false narratives that other people create about you will not have a hold on your life. When you have deeper relationship connections, meaningful career opportunities, and healthy emotional well-being, you won't alter your values, gifts, or purpose—because you will always remember who you are.

WAYS TO BEGIN ANCHORING YOURSELF
IN WHO YOU ARE

- Check in with your values before making a major decision.

- Reject opinions from others when you've already decided what you want.

- Create your own timeline for your life and adjust it to align with your capacity as needed.

Whenever someone asks for my advice on a decision they have to make or changes they are trying to create in their lives, I always respond with *How will the things you are deliberating over impact your purpose?* or *What version of yourself feels the most authentic?* Pointing them back in the direction of themselves prevents the truth of who they are from being tainted even by what I think.

OUR RESISTANCE TO REMEMBERING
WHO WE ARE

I wish I could say that remembering who I am has been easy. It hasn't always been enough to just talk with God about my life or to reflect on the experiences that led me to where I am today. There have been times when it was difficult to reconcile the truth of who I was with the truth of my circumstances. There have been times when who I was at my core was overshadowed by who I had to be, when I needed to survive. There have been times when experiences and responsibilities called forth a version of me that I was trying to outgrow. And there have been times when I desired to be so loved and accepted that I ended up straying so far from my core, and eventually didn't recognize myself.

I know I'm not the only one who has experienced this resistance. I see those times as a disconnect from my true self. And you may have experienced a disconnect as well.

By disconnect, I mean detached, estranged, or mentally and emotionally checked out from yourself. This can happen for the reasons I shared above, like a difficult circumstance you had to survive, but you may also disconnect from yourself if

You were raised to ignore or dismiss your true feelings. Children are often taught to be seen and not heard, girls and women are often encouraged to keep sweet and stay soft, and boys and men are often programmed to believe that showing any emotion besides anger or any virtue besides strength is weakness.

You learned to censor your true self. Experiences like rejection, bullying, abuse, or neglect may create a habit of shrinking, hiding, or masking. You can lose sight of yourself when you constantly switch up your identity, personality, or even your physical appearance because you don't feel safe, loved, or accepted when you are true to who you are.

You chose reckless rebellion. Being at war with others over who you are can put you at war with yourself. In an effort to prove you are different, ambitious, and deserving, you may take things too far—and stray from the values that are aligned with your true nature. You may find yourself relentlessly pursuing your idea of success and happiness at the expense of your reputation and character.

While I was working as a counselor in a correctional facility, I saw how the consequences of those kinds of disconnects could play out. I taught a four-week life skills course to hundreds of incarcerated men. A large portion of the curriculum was devoted to helping the inmates uncover positive skills, talents, and behaviors that would help them successfully reintegrate back into society.

Inmates can be labeled as antisocial because their criminal acts go against positive societal norms. As someone who grew up under the same conditions as many of these incarcerated men, I know that the norms of our society aren't always positive. These men didn't start out as criminals. They saw behaviors and patterns like addiction, violence, and other survival responses modeled by adults in their lives, and those patterns became their inheritance. So their behavior is not just something to punish but a deeper social issue that requires healing.

At the start of the first class, I always opened by asking, "Who did you want to be when you grew up?" The answers would vary. Some people said they wanted to be a lawyer, a doctor, or "I don't remember." But one answer was common for more than half the class: "No one"—most of the incarcerated men in class said they didn't want to be anyone when they grew up.

This sort of response didn't surprise me. One inmate shared how his uncle put a loaded gun in his hand when he was just seven years old and took him on his first robbery. Another shared how his mother put him to work at age ten because he was now the man of the house.

These men didn't have the luxury of dreaming of who they wanted to be. Everything in their experience made it seem like life was happening *to* them, with no regard for their own preferences or needs. The norms in their society were struggle, deficit, and loss. They responded to those things in the only ways that they knew how. They let life write their narratives, casting them as victims and eventually convicted criminals.

OVERCOMING OUR INTERNAL AND EXTERNAL RESISTANCES

I'm never surprised when someone shares that a single circumstance birthed the beliefs and behaviors that are hurting them now. It could be that a mother, teacher, or friend had projected their own negative beliefs and behaviors onto them as an impressionable child, or even when they were in a particularly vulnerable season as an adult. As a result, they made choices to help them cope with their circumstances and survive. Perhaps their family was struggling with money and they wanted to help, so they stole, sold drugs, or became a worker for someone else who was doing those things—because that's what was either modeled around them or what they were told to do.

Depending on how you grew up, these examples may sound extreme. Most likely, you were not given a gun by a family member at age seven. But perhaps someone you loved put a computer, baseball, or musical instrument in your hand and expected you to follow their plan for your life. Maybe you were expected to go into the family business, be married by a certain age, have children, or continue in your family's cultural traditions. These kinds of expectations can still keep you from the truth of who you are.

To help the students in my life skills class differentiate projections and their own voices, I asked them a series of questions: *Whose voice do you hear telling you that you will never be anything in life? Whose voice do you hear telling you that a life of crime is the only path to survival? Whose voice do you hear telling you that violence is the only way to earn respect?* Then I paused and asked a final question: *Is that voice a credible source?*

* * *

Take a moment to ask those questions of yourself.

> Whose voice do you hear telling you to be married by
> thirty, have the house with the picket fence, or achieve
> other status-centered forms of success?
> Whose voice do you hear telling you that you are not pretty,
> smart, or good enough?
> Whose voice do you hear telling you you're not easy to
> love?
> Whose voice do you hear telling you who you should be in
> life? Is that voice a credible source?

If you weren't nurtured as a child, you might constantly be looking outside of yourself to find what you've been missing. You'll find yourself waiting for permission, being defined by others, and doing things for attention and approval.

Overcoming this internal resistance looks like finding ways to bring joy, excitement, peace, love, and purpose into your life. Think about what you are doing when you feel those emotions, and do more of that each day. Uncover your gifts and learn to be skilled at them. Nurture yourself in ways you may never have experienced and create habits that your inner child would enjoy.

Every time you nurture yourself, you are remembering who you are.

Overcoming a Lack of Nurturing Can Look Like

- Wearing the clothes you like because you like them

- Requesting your favorite song during a car ride

- Being willing to be the only one with your point of view

- Joyfully exploring new ideas as they come up

- Honoring gut feelings without waiting for an endorsement from an outside source

It's important to note that the external projections we are trying to resist aren't always loud and obvious. Sometimes they are passive, like your parents' constant praise of your sibling, your boss promoting your co-worker, or your friend hanging out with a new friend. Your people choosing other people can low-key inspire you to want to alter who you are to align with who you think they want. When we don't notice and resist the passive circumstances in our lives that lead us to alter who we are, our self-esteem can start to slip easily, and we can begin engaging in self-sabotaging behavior. That's why it's important to maintain habits that root us in our own values, so we can get back on track easily when we stray from our core selves.

WHY REMEMBERING WHO YOU ARE MATTERS

Remembering who you are is not a universal habit. As with most things, it will look different for everyone, and it will require different practices depending on what made you forget who you were in the first place. We've discussed some of the reasons we may disconnect from our true selves and forget some of the amazing gifts that are inside us. And we've uncovered some of the internal consequences and negative emotions we feel when that happens.

But what's at stake when you forget who you are is the power you have to create the meaningful life you deserve.

People who forget who they are often settle in their relationships and careers. They live below their potential and refrain from pursuing goals and realizing their dreams. They often forfeit their opportunities and resign themselves to a life they deem as good enough. They may feel powerless, and hopeless, and experience diminished psychological fortitude (PF) because they see themselves as less than or small compared to their circumstances.

It is not always easy to identify when you have strayed or forgotten who you are. You may not be fully aware of the disconnect and describe yourself as feeling "off," unmotivated, unworthy, or—a common one I hear (and have said myself)—*lost*.

Here are some signs that you have forgotten who you are:

- You have resigned yourself to a life you didn't choose.

- You have settled for less than you deserve.

- You give up easily for fear of failure or judgment.

- You censor yourself to be accepted.

- You lack motivation and are bored with your life.

Remembering who you are is a preventative habit, but it is also the remedy to feeling lost, less than, and unsure of yourself.

There is another reason that the habit of remembering and honoring who you are matters. Sometimes we are guilty of trying to pass off self-betrayal as self-improvement. You may need to address this behavior in your own life if you have been hiding or trying to erase any parts of yourself to be accepted or to get ahead. Maybe you have started making changes that appear to be positive enhancements, like working out, cutting your hair, buying a new car, or moving to a new city. But if those things were done in response to a breakup, or to compete with recent accomplishments of your siblings, friends, or colleagues—and they are not inspired by a core desire to fulfill your own purpose, you're not acting in the interest of self-improvement—you're engaging in self-betrayal.

It can sometimes be good when you are inspired by others to make changes, but changing to compete or compare with others is problematic.

If you think this may be you, try answering these questions

- Whose voice do you hear telling you that you should change?

- What inspired your goal to lose weight, cut your hair, or whatever change you want to make?

- Are you trying to improve yourself or erase parts of who you are?

When you are unhappy with who you are, embarrassed by your circumstances, or conditioned to believe that who you are in name, deed, color, gender, and likeness isn't worthy of receiving positive things like professional opportunities, personal fortune, or your voice being heard—you may feel a temptation to alter who you are. Anchoring yourself in a remembrance of who you are helps you resist that temptation and show up fully as yourself.

The habit of remembering who you are ensures that your truest self is always present. Even when you do eventually make changes to improve your life—like going to college, getting a job, or moving to a new city—the real you should always be the one who shows up.

WHAT REMEMBERING WHO WE ARE
HEALS IN US

Maybe you've never had the emotional space, judgment-free opportunity, or personal freedom to decide who you are. You might know what it's like to play the role of child, sibling, friend, partner, or parent—but the possibility of being yourself, without all those labels, feels foreign.

One of my clients told me that our sessions were the only time anyone addressed her by her first name. At home, she was "Mom" or "Babe." At work, everyone went by their last name. She and her siblings referred to one another as "Sis" or "Bro." Her only living parent referred to her by her nickname (Belle). She felt like she had been who people expected her to be for so long that she had no identity outside of that.

A habit like asking to be referred to by your name may seem frivolous to some. But your name is how you are identified in every setting you walk into. It goes on every application, notice, email, and asset you own. Your name matters.

When we practice the habit of remembering who we are, we heal our relationship with possibility. There is more to you than the role you play in the lives of others. There are so many things that you get to decide for yourself that you may never have thought were possible.

You get to choose

- Your core beliefs and values

- If/when you want to be in a relationship

- Boundaries you need to feel safe and comfortable

- The career path you should take

- If you want to be a parent

- The traditions you want to keep or leave behind

- The name you want to answer to in life

I use this list annually, on my birthday, to decide who I want to be during the next year of my life. A few years ago, I decided that I would be an author. You are reading this book because I believed in the possibility of the person I saw in those daydreams all those years ago.

REMEMBERING WHO YOU ARE AND RECLAIMING YOUR POWER

In the introduction of this book, I related that when I was ten years old, I set a goal to get out of the hood. When I go back to that day, I can still remember sitting on those metal folding chairs at the community assembly I was attending for at-risk youth. I don't remember everything the speaker said that day, but toward the end of her speech, she started to share some facts, and I remember them clear as day:

If your parents were teenagers, the risk of you being a teenage parent is high. If you live in a home that exposes you to substance abuse, you will likely grow up abusing substances. If you're in an environment where there is domestic violence or violence of any kind, you are more likely to engage in violence or be a victim of it. If your parents or family members are incarcerated or have ever been to prison, you can end up in prison one day, too.

Sheesh. *Why is this woman telling my business?* I thought. I had experienced every single one of those circumstances. Teenage pregnancy, drug and alcohol abuse, violence, and incarceration were all part of my family's history. But as she ticked through all of those possible outcomes, my second thought was *Tuh! Not me.* The history of my grandparents, parents, aunts, uncles, and other relatives was their story, *not* mine.

All throughout my childhood, I remember daydreaming and seeing glimpses of an entirely different life. I saw myself as an adult, smiling as I walked into a room full of strangers seated in metal folding chairs just waiting for me. I saw myself as a student in college. I saw myself standing on a stage looking out at an audience. I had so many dreams and visions of living a happy and fulfilled life. I knew there had to be some divine reason I saw those glimmers of what was possible. I knew there was a greater plan for my life.

The habit of remembering who you are not only keeps you connected to the dreams and goals that light you up and inspire you to want to be the best version of yourself; it also keeps you connected to the power you already have inside you to make those dreams and goals a reality. You reclaim that power every time you remember that you have a unique purpose and calling. You reclaim your power every time you remember you have the skills and talents needed to be whoever you want to be in life.

My faith has always been at the center of my life. As a kid, I would talk with God often, and these conversations built up a strength and hope inside my soul. Even still, my prayers were layered with questions. I wondered how and when my dream of a fulfilled life would ever come true, since I was the child of a family that had made so many mistakes. But in my heart, I believed that I was God's child, too. His divine plan was also part of my story. The speaker was right about what could happen—statistically—to someone with my background, but my faith gave me the strength to reclaim my power and change the narrative of what could happen, and create my own outcomes.

Even when I was young, I knew that my faith had to be backed by actions and habits. As the speaker closed out her message, I closed my eyes and promised myself that I would not be who others called me. I decided that I would live according to my own standards, not someone's statistics. I decided to take action to get out of the hood, not be a teenage parent, and not be a victim of domestic violence. Then and there, I made a choice to write my own story and enhance my family's history.

Even if you're well past the age of ten, you can reclaim your own power by remembering who you are and deciding what happens from this point on. You may need to unlearn some things, reject some traditions, break some cycles, and tap into a divine force for change. But you get to define and decide for yourself.

I can't have a conversation about knowing or remembering who you are without sharing this declaration: *You are who God created you to be and nothing less. Good things are going to happen to you, through you, and for you.*

The habit of remembering who you are begins with your decision to be who you were created to be. Going against who others have defined you as, carving out space to heal who you had to be in the past, and coming home to yourself after self-betrayal and denial—these acts take courage and faith.

Make time to entertain your daydreams and visions. Seeing yourself in the future is a divine gift. Let yourself be hopeful about who you can be. Give yourself permission to believe and have faith.

Once you decide who you want to be, you will have to back up that decision with daily habits that reinforce it. You will have to make that same decision to show up fully as yourself every day, in every circumstance, and often against the resistance of others.

FOUR STEPS TO BEGIN REMEMBERING
WHO YOU ARE

1. **Make decisions based on living, not surviving.** *Having to make decisions that you are not proud of to survive can give you a distorted view of yourself.* You may feel like you are being mean for distancing yourself in relationships to protect your heart, or unreliable because you have to back out of things when you feel too anxious. When you're in survival mode, you have to do things you wouldn't do otherwise. Under pressure, you may meet an anxious, moody, fearful, and overwhelmed version of yourself. Do not judge the version of yourself that you had to be to survive. When you are safe, find your way back to who you really are.

   Remembering who you are after survival will require practices that make you feel safe and comforted.

   Here are some specific habits to consider:

   • Entertaining new friendships inspired by your current interests

   • Creating a bucket list and committing to crossing off one thing a month or year

   • Exploring practices like deep breathing, meditation, and affirmations to manage anxiety

   • Dancing, running, painting, or doing other activities that bring you joy

   • Calling an old friend to reminisce about times when you felt confident or funny, or to remind yourself of other attributes you appreciated about yourself

2. **Surround yourself with people who really see you.**
   Being surrounded by people who don't see you can cause you to question your significance. Perhaps you don't feel like you can truly be yourself around your partner. You may fear that exposure to certain parts of your personality may scare them away. Or perhaps you feel like your job, special projects, or other details you want to share about your life are not as meaningful as your siblings'.

   Remembering who you are when no one sees you starts with seeing yourself. You might have to start celebrating small wins and acknowledging personal milestones. This may require you to root for yourself and hold yourself accountable for fulfilling your goals. But this also looks like being open to new people who share your values and interests, and cultivating relationships outside of your circle. When you know who you are and show up confidently as yourself, you will catch the attention of the people you are called to.

   The people you are called to are those who take a genuine interest in what you have to say. They value your opinion and respect your boundaries. They see your skills, talents, and gifts and encourage your efforts. They are not just aware of your significance; they help you see it as well.

   To attract these people into your life you will have to

   - Heal or bring an end to the relationships that make you question your worth

   - Own the unique, and maybe even quirky, parts of your personality

   - Share some aspects of the story of your life that set you apart from everyone else

- Be open to standing out in the crowd because you look or think differently

- Speak on principles and values that bring awareness to causes you believe in

3. **Don't get caught in the trap of comparison.** *Getting caught up in the comparison trap will strip you of your unique essence.* Instead of being who you are, you'll become an imitation of who you think someone else is. The most common things I've seen the people I work with compare themselves to are the relationships of their friends, the financial status of their siblings, the personality and/or body of the current partner of an ex, and the lifestyle of someone they follow on social media. Remember, you may not have the whole story of someone else's life or the things they had to go through to get to where they are.

One way to escape this trap is by exploring what you are comparing yourself to, or what you are jealous of. This may sound counterintuitive, but it's actually a great practice to increase self-awareness and self-actualization. Admitting you are jealous of a sibling can help you uncover a hidden interest.

Try creating a list of the people you compare yourself to, and the reasons why. You may include things like money, looks, or relationships. Once you've compiled your list, explore ways you can create those things in your own life. How can you earn more money, improve your looks, or enhance your relationship? What do you need to stop or start doing? When can you begin to make that happen? This is not about mimicking someone else's life but rather being inspired by it.

4. **Identify your values, and prioritize your heart's desires.** *Betraying your own heart by making decisions that distance you from the truth of who you are will eventually make you unrecognizable.* If you've ever looked around at your life and felt lost, it's because you've strayed from your own beliefs, values, and purpose in life. Engaging in habits like survival, people-pleasing, and comparison for too long will make you lose sight of what you care about. Lying about how you feel prevents you from getting your needs met. And when your needs go unmet, you can become bitter, resentful, angry, and frustrated. Those emotions often lead to behavior that doesn't resemble who you believe yourself to be.

Going against your standards puts your purpose at risk. You end up aligning with people and things that stunt your growth. You settle. You forfeit opportunities to realize your full potential. It's not that you don't know who you are—you've just buried the truth of it behind someone else's.

Start identifying your values, uncovering your needs, and prioritizing your heart's desires. You can ease into this process by spending an entire day speaking only the truth. Try practicing this in small ways, like being honest when someone asks how you're doing. You don't have to disclose private matters, but you could start with a small truth like, "I am looking forward to a weekend of rest" instead of the universal response of "Good." Or when someone is having a conversation you are uncomfortable with, honor your personal conviction by saying, "I don't agree, so I am probably not the best person for you to have this conversation with."

Remembering who you are isn't about maintaining a

perfect version of yourself. It's finding the courage to reclaim your power and truly be who you are—even when it's uncomfortable, confrontational, bold, and different from everyone else. The truth of who you are can be layered, it can be messy, it can be troubled, and it can be lost inside of the life that you are trying desperately to build. But remembering who you are is making a commitment to always find your way back to yourself.

PROMPTS FOR REMEMBERING WHO YOU ARE

In what areas of your life do you need to remember who you are? Are there parts of yourself that you shrink or hide to be accepted or make others comfortable? Have you forgotten your talents, gifts, or skills? Have you allowed your circumstances or other people to define you?

Why do you need to remember who you are? Will remembering who you are help you create a life that is meaningful, honest, and expansive? Will remembering who you are help you to stop settling?

What does remembering who you are look like? Will you be more honest about what you want in life? Will you ask for the promotion or start the business? Will you stop allowing others to project their beliefs onto you?

How will you practice the habit of remembering who you are today, this week, and/or this month? What are the actions you can commit to doing? Even if it shocks others, can you choose the job, the move, or the family you've always wanted? Can you reflect on ways you've betrayed yourself and take steps to self-correct? Can you make a new list of values and standards?

USE THE SPACE BELOW TO WORK
THROUGH THE PROMPTS ON YOUR OWN

Need: _____

_____

_____

Why do I need to do this? _____

_____

_____

Healing Habits: _____

_____

_____

Practices/Action: _____

_____

_____

AFFIRMATIONS FOR REMEMBERING WHO YOU ARE

Say this out loud with me:

I am who God created me to be and nothing less.
I have a right to take up space.
Who I am is good enough.
I honor the work that I put in to get here.
I am deserving of good things.

A WORD ON HEALING

When I first came to the realization that I needed healing, I remember feeling frustrated. I thought it was unfair that I had to repair damage that I didn't cause and didn't deserve, all in order to experience a life that I felt I should have been living already. As I moved through my healing process, I grew even angrier. I was doing the work and *still* experiencing struggles. It wasn't that I expected a perfect life—no one gets that—but I certainly didn't expect the struggle to be so hard.

A client once told me that her healing process felt like a game of hide-and-seek. One minute her healing was in plain sight and within her reach, the next minute she felt like she was running around in circles trying to find peace of mind.

I could relate.

My daughter used to have this habit of leaving a game of hide-and-seek with her father to come sit near me at the computer, on the sofa, or in the kitchen. This happened almost every time they played the game. When I asked her if she had found her father, she would say, "No, I'm not playing anymore." When I asked why, she would say he was too hard to find, or she was scared to look in places like the closet or basement. I'd let her sit with me for a while and then would encourage her not to give up. I reminded her that no matter how long it took, she always found him. And the house belonged to her, so she had already been in the basement and every closet many times. There was nothing new to fear.

We don't talk enough about the fact that healing is something you have to work at every day, even if only in small ways. Deserving to be healed, wanting to be healed, and praying to be healed are not enough. Healing starts there, but it progresses only because of your daily participation. You will have to work for it, really hard at times. You may also have to heal more than once from the same thing. More than one person may break your heart. More than one family member may try to test your boundaries. Trauma from your past may show up in the form of triggers, time and time again. You may lose sight of who you are several times in your lifetime.

But you can't cheat the process. You can't predict where the journey will lead you. You can't regulate the ebbs and flows, and you can't control how someone else responds to the healed version of you. What you *can* control is your response. Every time you respond with a positive habit in the face of struggle, you reclaim your purpose, your peace, and your power.

Every time it hurts, heal again.

Through habits like the ones in this book, you will find the healing you've been looking for. And when you get frustrated or angry about how hard it feels, remind yourself that you are healing things that you have already lived through and survived. When life gets too busy or you find yourself in the thick of struggle, encourage yourself to keep working for your healing. Tapping into these habits is how you will find your way back to wholeness and positive well-being.

The habits for healing we have discussed will not free you from every struggle, but they will empower you to overcome them. When your purpose is secured, your peace is intact, and you are standing in your power, you can always find your way to a place of healing.

There was one other thing I would say to my daughter when she wanted to give up hide-and-seek. I'd say, "Your father isn't hiding from you—he's waiting for you to find him."

Your healing is not out of view or out of reach. It isn't running from you or hiding. You aren't disqualified from it because your wounds happened in the past. You can start the process over as many times as you need to get it right.

My hope is that somewhere in this book—a single page, a particular chapter, a story that spoke to you—you found something that will help you heal, grow, and become the person you are meant to be.

Go at your own pace, taking things in little by little or all at once. You may have read this book and decided to start with boundaries instead of self-care because that's what you need to work through right now. You may have enjoyed the stories more than the practices in your first read-through because you needed to be reminded of specific moments in your own life. You may prefer to take immediate action, so you gave special attention to the prompts, even stopped for a week or two to put each habit to work in your life before moving on to the next chapter.

"You are an expert on you," as my therapist likes to say.

In this book I've shared my story and stories from my clients, as well as my philosophy and advice. *Now it's your turn.* Use the prompts at the end of each chapter to develop your own customized plan for healing with the habits you're ready for. And remember, when you put the book down, you can always pick right back up where you left off.

As we close this journey together, I want to leave you with a prayer like the ones that I have shared with my online audience every Sunday for the past six years. Today, this prayer is for you:

I pray you go from self-sacrifice to self-care.

I pray you emotionally release and let go of everything that has you stuck in sameness.

I pray you take accountability for the role you play in your own struggle and start rewriting your own story.

I pray you grow to accept what you can't change and fix what you can.

I pray you forgive yourself for learning some things the hard way.

I pray the things you used to take personally become things you use to become better.

I pray that minding your own business gives you the physical and emotional freedom you need to create a life you love.

I pray you find the courage to set boundaries that secure your peace.

I pray you remember you.

Acknowledgments

My journey to the work I am currently doing in the world started with some of the stories you just read. Those stories inspired lessons I started sharing with friends and family via random emails more than fourteen years ago. Syreena saw value in those lessons, encouraged me to start a blog, and eventually built my first website. I am not sure I'd be an author if she hadn't lent me her time and talent. Syreena, I am forever grateful for you.

I had a private Instagram account that I used to keep up with my family back home. I would share excerpts from my blog there from time to time. Destiney told me I was "playing small" and introduced me to the world of online influencing. Thank you for your contribution to my journey, Beloved.

Every like, share, comment, and DM from those who share space with me on social media has led to opportunities that have allowed my words to live in the hearts of people from around the world. My books are on shelves in countries I have yet to visit personally. That is a blessing I am still trying to find enough ways to show gratitude for. Thank you for being brave enough to hear hard truths, do hard work, and heal and grow through hard times.

May you, my amazing readers, followers, and community, never forget that you are worth healing for.

To write this book, I had to become a version of myself that I never knew existed. Thank you, Kanya, for reminding me that I have always been who I am. To Charity for being a consistent voice in my life. I hear you when I need to extend myself grace and when I need to apply more pressure. Whenever I have reached a new level in my life, your voice was in the background saying things I'd never let you say on speakerphone. I love you like a sister. To Lyn (Ms. Lyn, Dr. Lyn), thank you for seeing me when all I wanted to do was hide. Thank you for trusting me with your story and reading every word of mine during this process. You have been the friend I didn't know I needed. To Alison, thank you for being an ally and a refreshing source of laughter and joy when I was trying to decide if "this" was something I actually wanted.

To my Sissy, there are no words . . . You have always been my motivation. To my sisters, brothers, nieces, nephews, and cousins, our layered stories are uniquely divine. Everything I do has your imprint on it. We are all proof that good can come from the hood. I do it all for us.

To my children, thank you for being #teammom while I worked on this book and everything else I do. Your patience, mini celebrations, and presence gave me ease under pressure. Thank you, Chase, for always asking how it was coming along. Thank you, Kai, for listening to me work out chapters and decide on stories. May the things you learn about me in this book provide more context to our relationship. Long before you arrived in the flesh, you were in my heart. I named you, wrote to you, worked to break cycles for you, and started parts of this healing journey for you. May the result be generational healing and positive well-being.

Thank you, Charles, for checking in. Thank you, Yvonne, for every single "Good Morning, Gorgeous" text and for *seeing* that this was possible when I was still only dreaming of it. Thank you to every mentor and every friend.

To my agent, Trinity McFadden, and her team at The Bindery, thank you for representing me and my voice so well. To my Convergent and Penguin Random House team, thank you for contributing so intently to this work. To my editor, Derek Reed, you saw the vision from the beginning and helped me turn the story of the green string my grandmom tied around my neck into a complete work. Thank you for your prompts for deeper reflection. To Leita Williams for the careful considerations that helped me compose thoughts and harmonize my work. Both you and Derek helped me become a better writer. To Rachel Tockstein and Alisse Goldsmith-Wissman, my incredible marketer and publicist at Convergent, thank you for all the hard work you put into my book's launch.

To God, thank you for it all. Through every struggle, every goal accomplished, every loss, every mistake, every word written, and every word unspoken, you have remained. Thank you for choosing me to do this work and empowering me to fulfill this call. My answer will forever be "yes."

To my dad for always reminding me that I could do hard things. We loved hard even through hard times. To my grandmom, whose presence rests on every one of these pages, forever and always. See you in my dreams.

About the Author

NAKEIA HOMER is a well-being and mental health educator and a self-healing guide. She teaches her own executive education course at the David Eccles School of Business, University of Utah. Through programs, speaking, workshop facilitation, and corporate wellness consulting, she helps people sustain their well-being, operate in their brilliance, and show up in their lives and work as the best versions of themselves. She is the author of *I Hope This Helps* and *All the Right Pieces* and the founder of Heal & Grow Daily, a self-healing community and membership program. As a sought-after wellness and well-being expert and trauma-informed educator, Homer facilitates powerful workshops and keynotes on the power of acceptance, self-love/self-care, and purpose.

nakeiahomer.com
Facebook.com/nakeiahomer
X: @nakeiahomer
Instagram: @nakeiahomer

About the Type

This book was set in Berkeley, a typeface designed by Tony Stan (1917–88) in the early 1980s. It was inspired by, and is a variation on, University of California Old Style, created in the late 1930s by Frederic William Goudy (1865–1947) for the exclusive use of the University of California at Berkeley. The present face, in fact, bears influences of a number of Goudy's fonts, including Kennerley, Goudy Old Style, and Deepdene. Berkeley is notable for both its legibility and its lightness.